Level 2 · Part 2

Integrated Chinese

中文听说读写
中文聽説讀寫

CHARACTER WORKBOOK
Simplified and Traditional Characters

THIRD EDITION BY

Yuehua Liu and Tao-chung Yao
Yaohua Shi, Liangyan Ge, Nyan-Ping Bi

CHENG & TSUI COMPANY
Boston

16 15 14 13 12   2 3 4 5 6 7 8 9 10

Published by
Cheng & Tsui Company, Inc.
25 West Street
Boston, MA 02111-1213 USA
Fax (617) 426-3669
www.cheng-tsui.com
"Bringing Asia to the World"™

ISBN 978-0-88727-694-1

Cover Design: studioradia.com

Cover Photographs: Man with map © Getty Images; Shanghai skyline © David Pedre/iStockphoto; Building with masks © Wu Jie; Night market © Andrew Buko. Used by permission.

Interior Design: hiSoft

Project Management: Laurel Damashek
Production: Victoria E. Kichuk
Manufacturing: JoAnne Sweeney
Proofreading: Laurel Damashek
Composition: hiSoft
Printing and Binding: Sheridan

The Integrated Chinese series includes books, workbooks, character workbooks, audio products, multimedia products, teacher's resources, and more. Visit www.cheng-tsui.com for more information on the other components of Integrated Chinese.

Printed in the United States of America.

CONTENTS

Preface

This completely revised and redesigned Character Workbook is meant to accompany the third edition of *Integrated Chinese* Level 2 *(IC 2)*. It has been over ten years since the *IC* series came into existence in 1923. During these years, amid all the historical changes that took place in China and the rest of the world, the demand for Chinese language teaching/ learning materials has grown dramatically. We are greatly encouraged by the fact that *IC* not only has been a widely used textbook at the college level all over the United States and beyond, but also has become increasingly popular for advanced language students in high schools. Based on user feedback, we have made numerous changes so that the Character Workbook can become an even more useful tool for students of Chinese.

Stressing the importance of learning a new character by its components

Learning a new character becomes much easier if the student can identify its components. If a new character contains a component already familiar to the student, the stroke order of that component will not be introduced again. However, we will show the stroke order of all new components as they appear when we introduce new characters. When the student learns a new character, he or she can easily tell if a component in the character has appeared in previous lessons. If the stroke order for that component is not displayed, it means that the component is not new. The student should try to recall where he or she has seen it before. By doing so, the student can connect new characters with old ones and build up a character bank. We believe that learning by association will help the student memorize characters better.

Main features of the new Character Workbook

a. Both traditional and simplified characters are introduced in equal size
If a character appears in both traditional and simplified forms, we show both to accommodate different learner needs.

b. Pinyin and English definition are clearly noted
We have moved the pinyin and the English definition above each character for easy recognition and review.

c. Radicals are highlighted
The radical of each character is highlighted. Knowing what radical group a character belongs to is essential when looking up that character in a traditional dictionary where the characters are arranged according to their radicals. To a certain extent, radicals can also help the student decipher the meaning of a character. For example, characters containing the radical 貝/贝 (bèi, shell), such as 貴/贵 (guì, expensive), and 貨/货 (huò, merchandise), are often associated with money or value. The student can group the characters sharing the same radical together and learn them by association.

d. Stroke order is prominently displayed

Another feature that we think is important is the numbering of each stroke in the order of its appearance. Each number is marked at the beginning of that particular stroke. We firmly believe that it is essential to write a character in the correct stroke order, and to know where each stroke begins and ends. To display the stroke order more prominently, we have moved the step-by-step character writing demonstration next to the main characters.

e. A "training wheel" is provided

We also provide grids with fine shaded lines inside to help the student better envision and balance their characters when practicing.

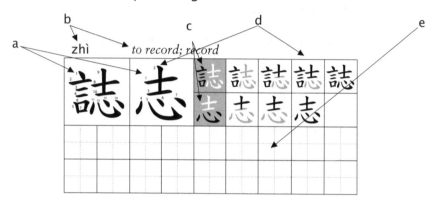

Other features in the new edition

A set of Chinese Character Crosswords has been added to each lesson. Students are asked to fill out the crossword puzzles based on the pinyin given, which helps them retain and re-associate characters when forming words.

To help the student look up characters more easily, we decided to provide two indices, one arranged alphabetically by pinyin and the other by lesson. The formation and radical of each character in this book are based on the fifth edition of the *Modern Chinese Dictionary* (現代漢語詞典第五版/现代汉语词典第五版) published by the Commercial Press (商務印書館/商务印书馆). A total of 201 radicals and the stroke number and stroke order of each character all appear in that dictionary, and in some cases the same character is listed under more than one radical. For the characters in this book that fall into that category, we provide two radicals in order to facilitate students' dictionary searches. The two radicals are presented in order from top to bottom (e.g., 名: 夕, 口), left to right (e.g., 功：工, 力), and large to small (e.g., 章: 音, 立; 麻: 麻, 广).

The changes that we made in the new version reflect the collective wishes of the users. We would like to take this opportunity to thank those who gave us feedback on how to improve the Character Workbook. We would like to acknowledge in particular Professor Hu Shuangbao of Beijing University, who read the entire manuscript and offered invaluable comments and suggestions for revision. Ms. Laurel Damashek at Cheng & Tsui assisted throughout the production process.

We hope you find this new edition useful. We welcome your comments and feedback. Please report any typos or other errors to **editor@cheng-tsui.com**.

Lesson 11

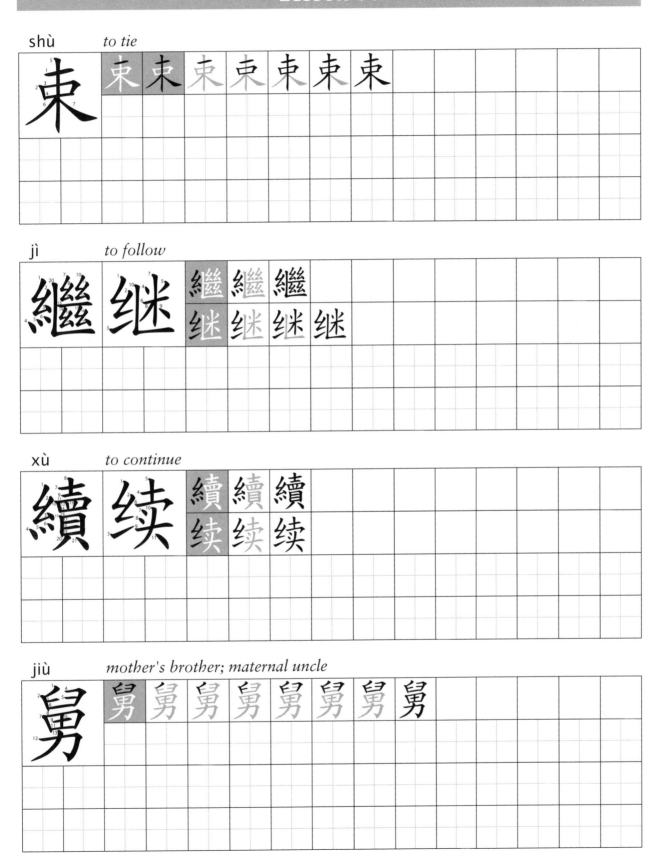

shù   *to tie*

束

jì   *to follow*

繼 继

xù   *to continue*

續 续

jiù   *mother's brother; maternal uncle*

舅

qū   *district*

區 区 區 區 區 區
区 区 区 区

huán   *ring; to surround*

環 环 環 環 環
环 环 环

jìng   *territory*

境 境 境 境 境 境

qiáng   *wall*

牆 墙 墙 墙 墙 墙 墙 墙 墙 墙 墙 墙
墙 墙 墙 墙 墙 墙 墙

tiē   *to paste; to glue*

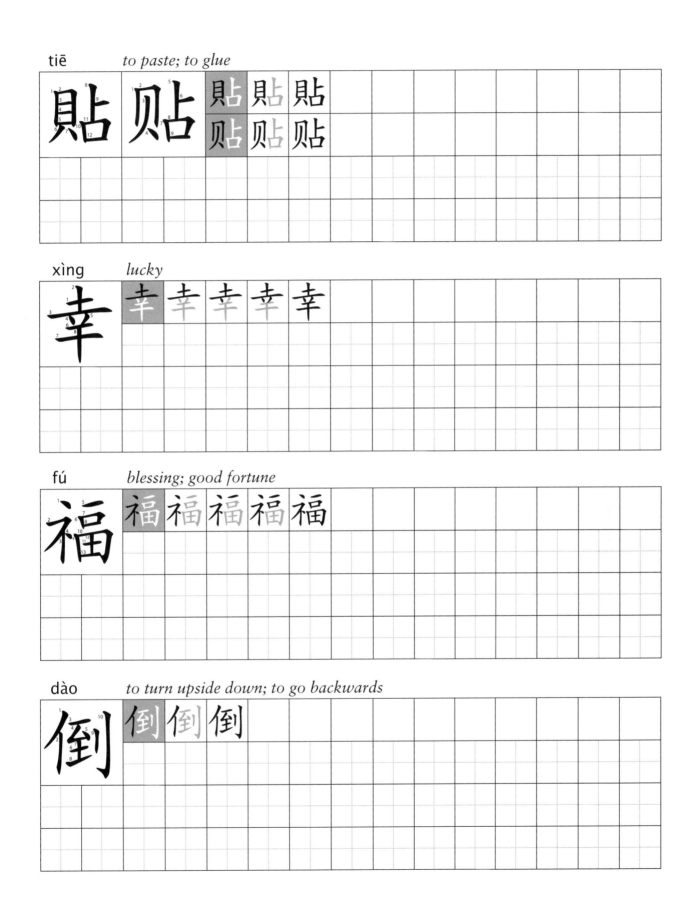

xìng   *lucky*

fú   *blessing; good fortune*

dào   *to turn upside down; to go backwards*

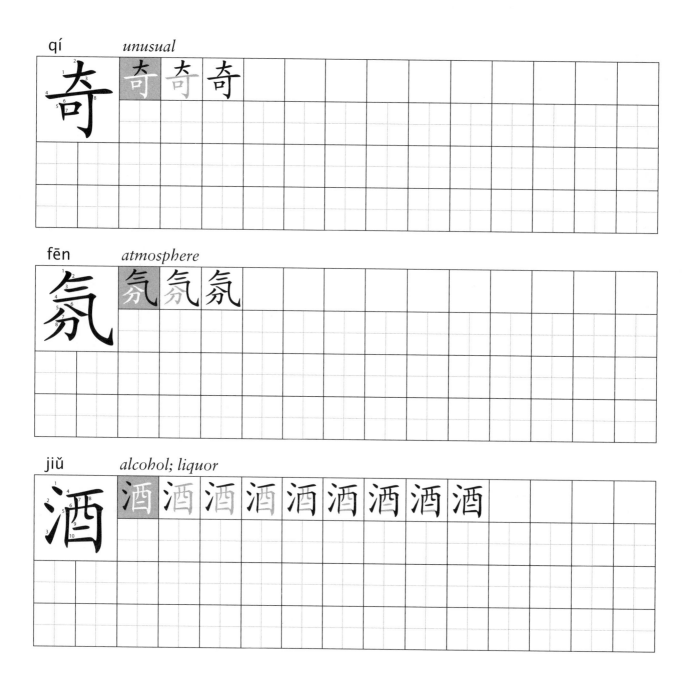

qí   *unusual*

奇

fēn   *atmosphere*

氛

jiǔ   *alcohol; liquor*

酒

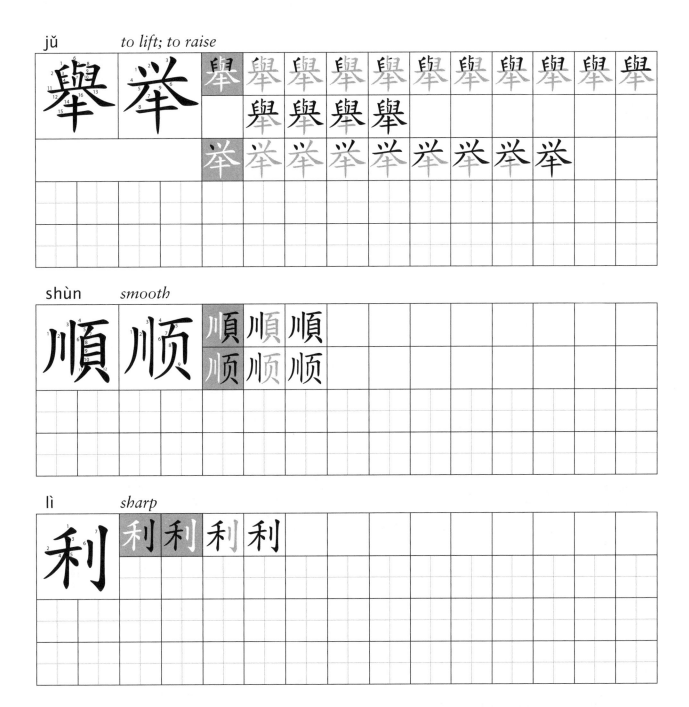

jǔ   *to lift; to raise*

shùn   *smooth*

lì   *sharp*

shèng   *to leave a surplus; to be left (over)*

剩   剩 剩 剩 剩 剩 剩 剩 剩 剩 剩 剩 剩

làng   *wave; unrestrained*

浪   浪 浪 浪

yú   *to surplus; to spare*

餘 余   餘 餘 餘 餘 餘 餘 餘 餘
　　　余 余 余 余 余 余 余

chuán   *to pass down; to transfer*

傳 传   傳 傳 傳
　　　传 传 传

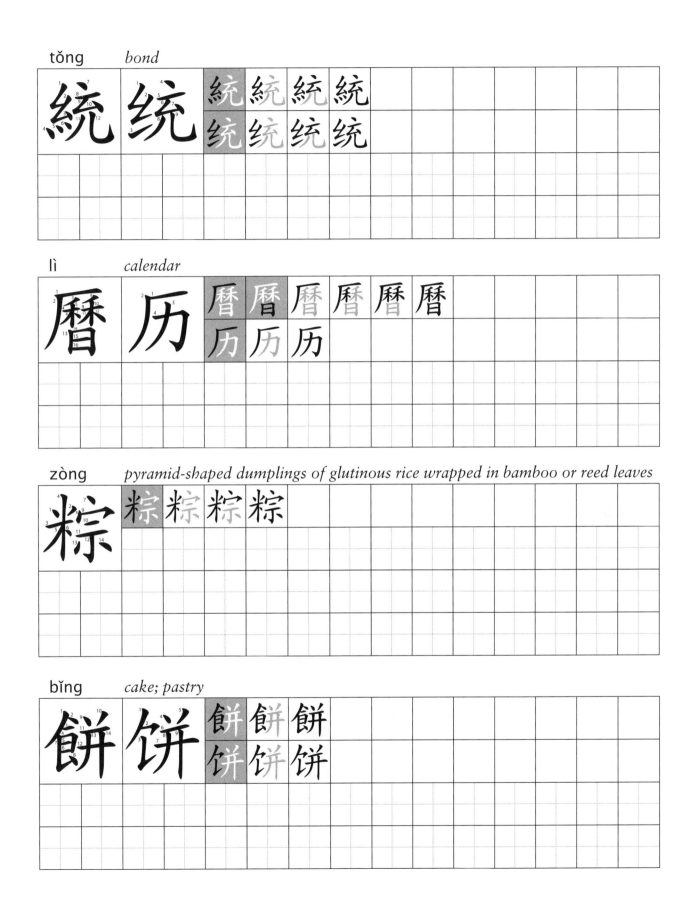

tǒng   *bond*

統 统

lì   *calendar*

曆 历

zòng   *pyramid-shaped dumplings of glutinous rice wrapped in bamboo or reed leaves*

粽

bǐng   *cake; pastry*

餅 饼

tuán   *sphere; lump*

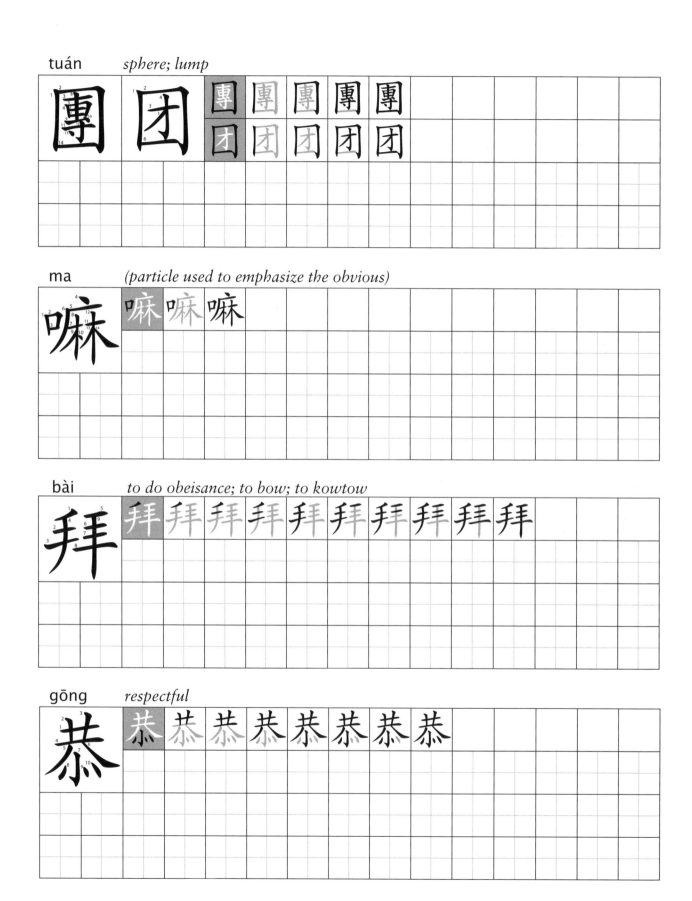

ma   *(particle used to emphasize the obvious)*

bài   *to do obeisance; to bow; to kowtow*

gōng   *respectful*

cái   *wealth*

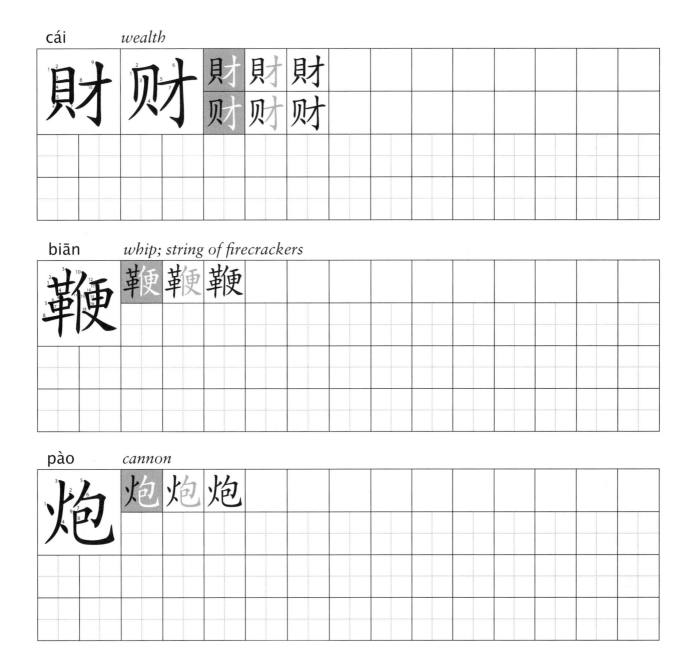

biān   *whip; string of firecrackers*

pào   *cannon*

Characters from Proper Nouns

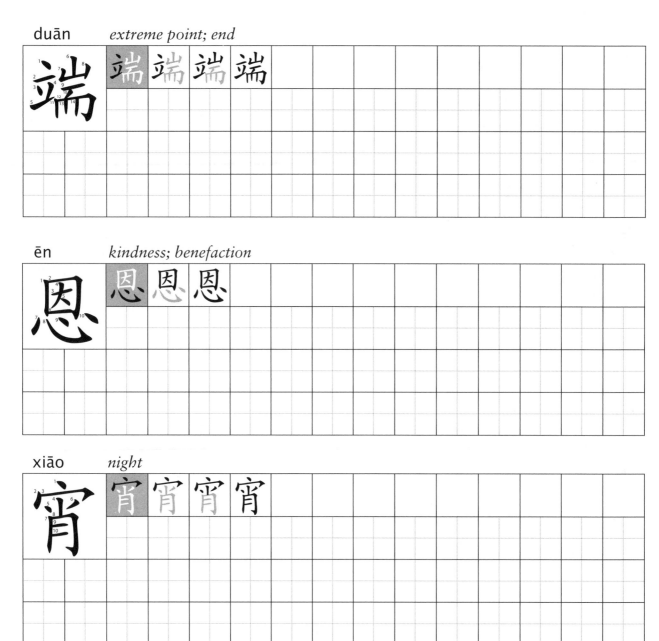

duān   *extreme point; end*

ēn   *kindness; benefaction*

xiāo   *night*

Chinese Character Crosswords

Fill out the puzzles based on the *pinyin* clues provided. The common character is positioned in the center of the cluster of rings. The arrows indicate which way you should read the words.

1.
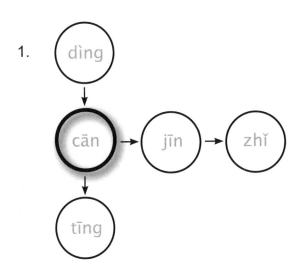

2.
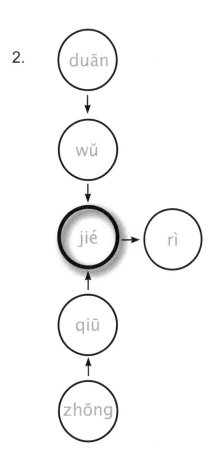

3.
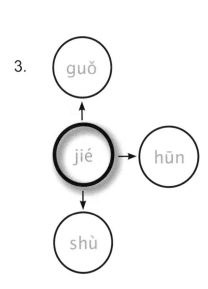

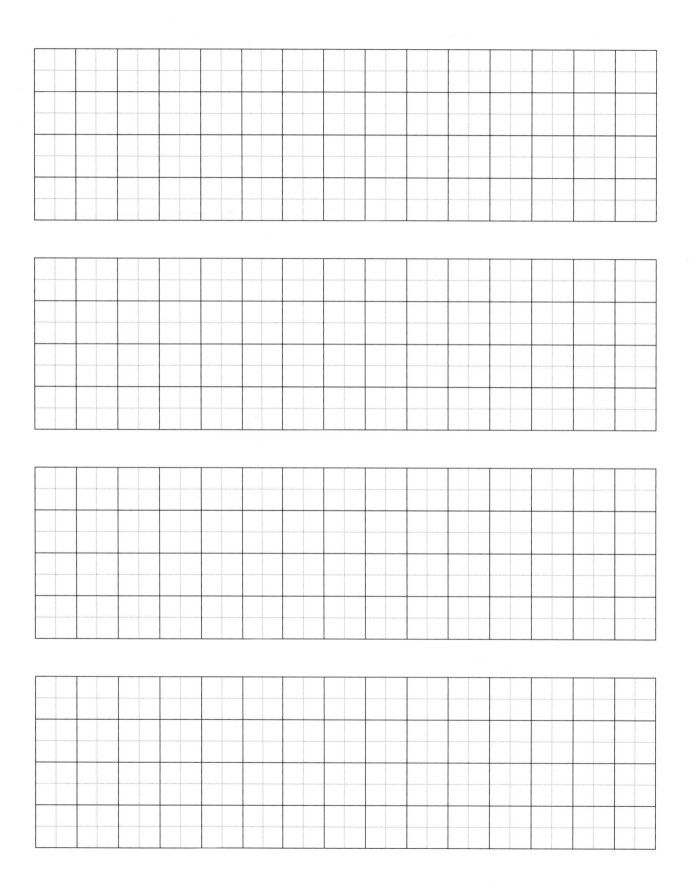

Lesson 12

biàn *to change*

変 变

jí *to reach; to come up to*

及

jìng *unexpectedly; contrary to one's expectation*

竟

gū *father's sister*

姑

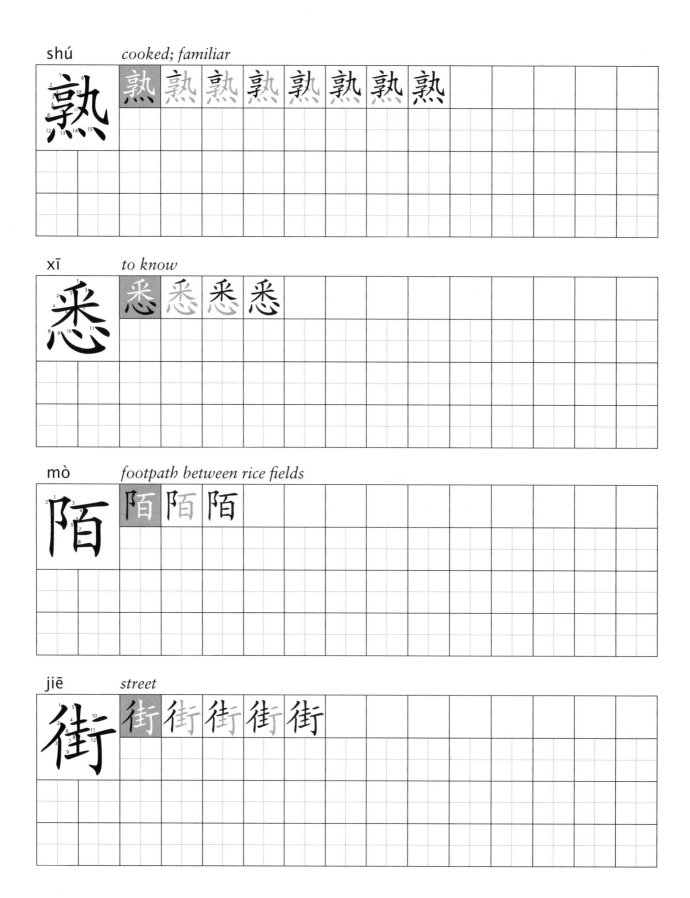

shú   *cooked; familiar*

xī   *to know*

mò   *footpath between rice fields*

jiē   *street*

gài   *to build; to construct*

蓋 盖 蓋 蓋 蓋 蓋
盖 盖 盖 盖 盖

què   *certain; true*

確 确 確 確 確 確 確 確 確 確 確 確
確
确 确 确

qí   *to ride*

騎 骑 騎 騎 騎
骑 骑 骑

zhuāng   *clothing*

裝　裝

築　筑

zhù   *to construct*

cháng   *to taste*

嚐　尝

jǐn   *to exhaust*

儘　尽

shà   *big building; mansion*

厦 厦 厦 厦 厦
厦 厦 厦

zuò   *(measure word for buildings and mountains)*

座 座 座 座

shēng   *sound*

聲 声 聲 聲 聲 聲 聲 聲 聲
声 声 声 声 声 声

gū   *to mumble; to rumble*

咕 咕 咕 咕

lū   *rumbling*

嚕 嚕 嚕嚕嚕嚕

Characters from Proper Nouns

fū   *man; male adult*

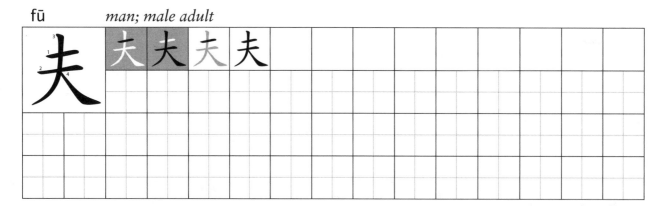

夫 夫夫夫夫

miào   *temple*

廟 庙 廟庙

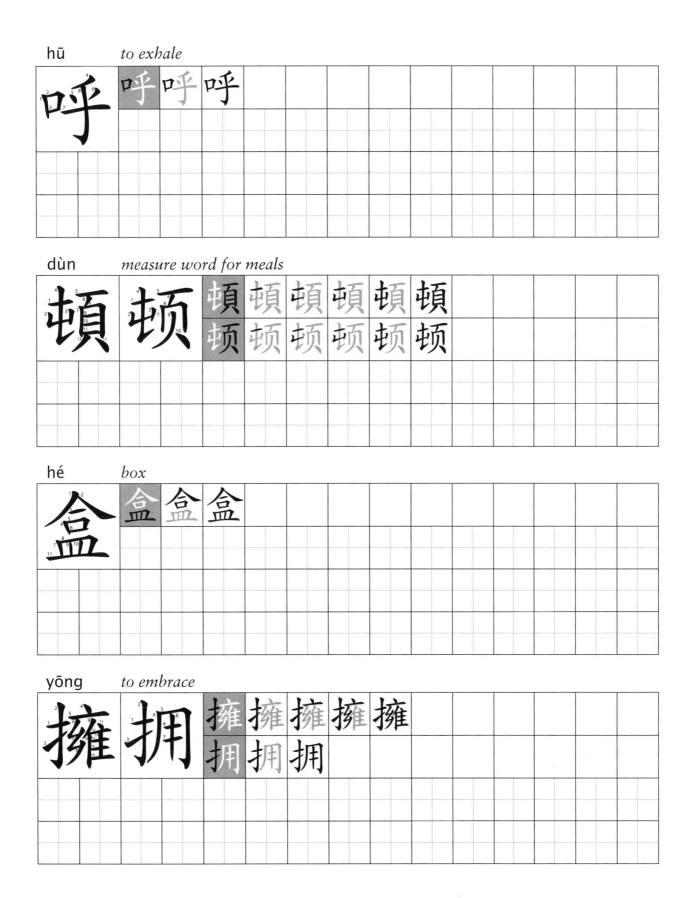

hū   *to exhale*
呼

dùn   *measure word for meals*
頓 顿

hé   *box*
盒

yōng   *to embrace*
擁 拥

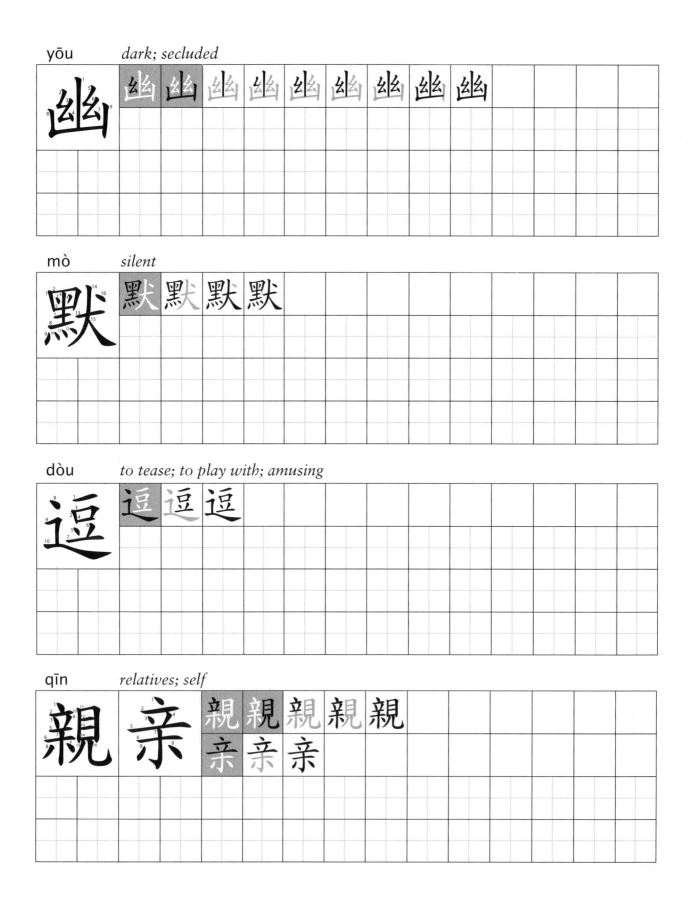

yōu   *dark; secluded*

幽

mò   *silent*

默

dòu   *to tease; to play with; amusing*

逗

qīn   *relatives; self*

親 亲

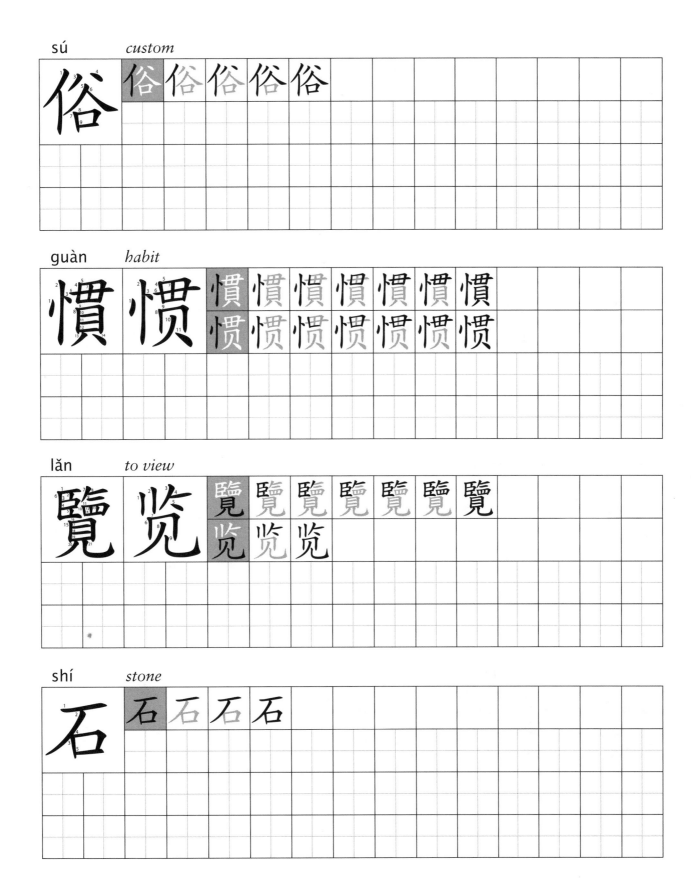

shù   *tree*

樹 树 樹 樹 樹 樹 樹 樹 樹
树 树 树 树

jiǎng   *to speak; to tell*

講 讲 講 講 講
讲 讲 讲 讲 讲 讲

gù   *ancient; former*

故 故 故 故

tǎ   *tower; pagoda-shaped structure*

塔 塔 塔 塔 塔
塔 塔 塔 塔

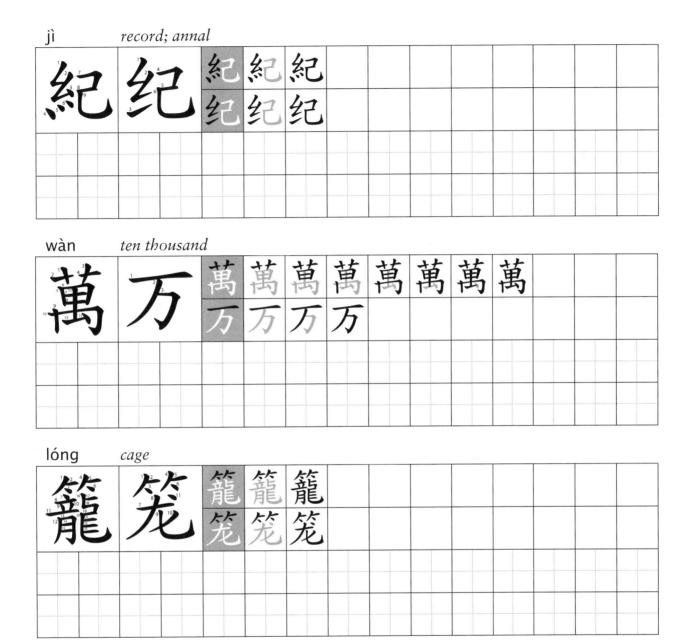

Character from Proper Nouns

kūn   *elder brother; descendant*

Chinese Character Crosswords

Fill out the puzzles based on the *pinyin* clues provided. The common character is positioned in the center of the cluster of rings. The arrows indicate which way you should read the words.

1.

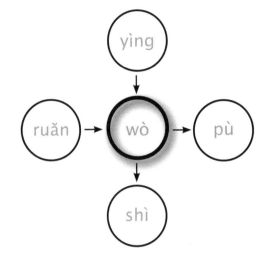

2.

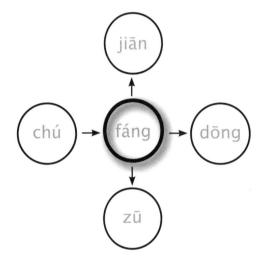

3.

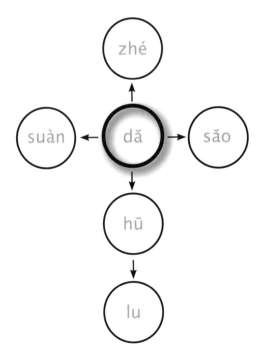

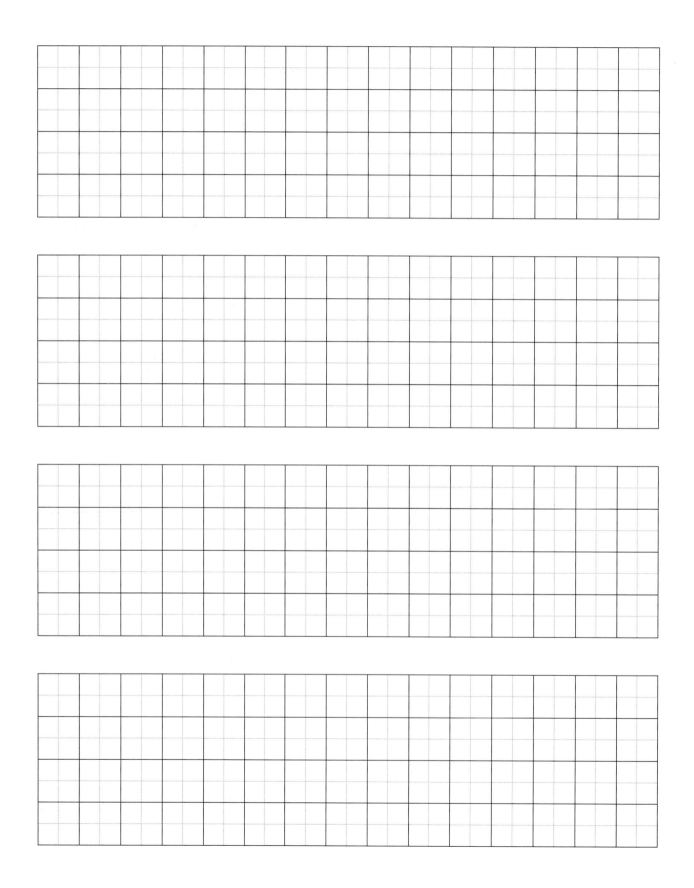

Lesson 14

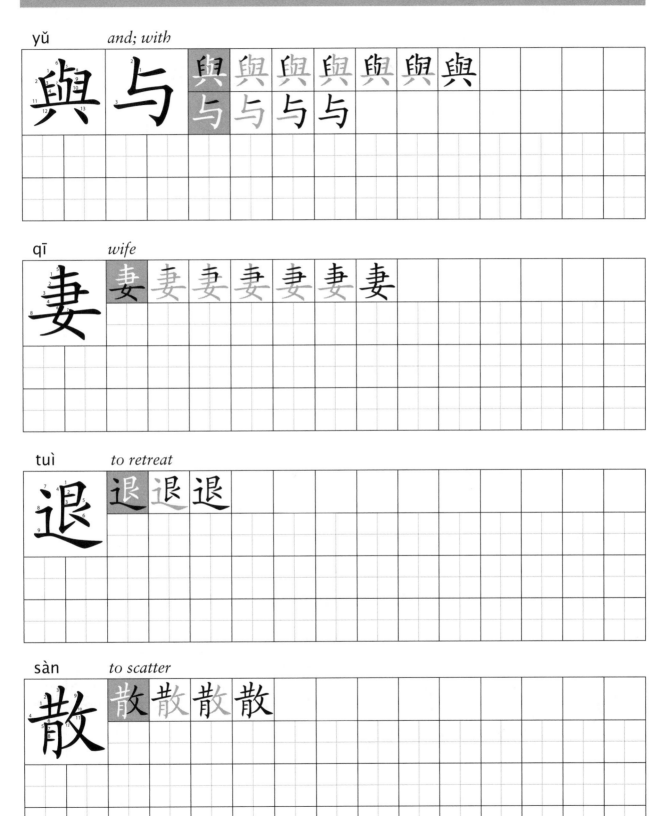

yǔ — *and; with*
與 与 | 與 與 與 與 與 與 | 与 与 与 与

qī — *wife*
妻 | 妻 妻 妻 妻 妻 妻 妻

tuì — *to retreat*
退 | 退 退 退

sàn — *to scatter*
散 | 散 散 散 散

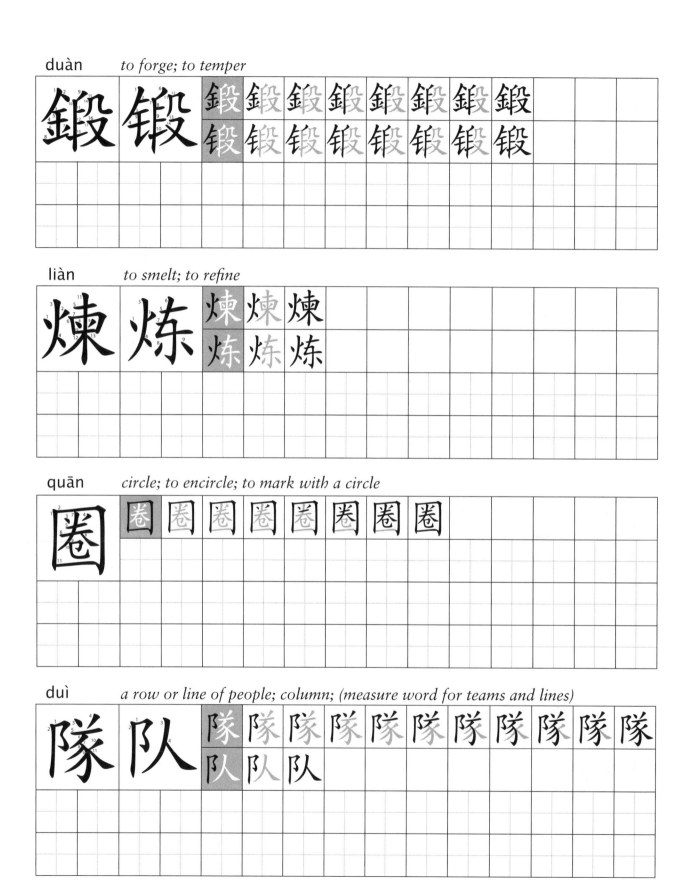

duàn — *to forge; to temper*

liàn — *to smelt; to refine*

quān — *circle; to encircle; to mark with a circle*

duì — *a row or line of people; column; (measure word for teams and lines)*

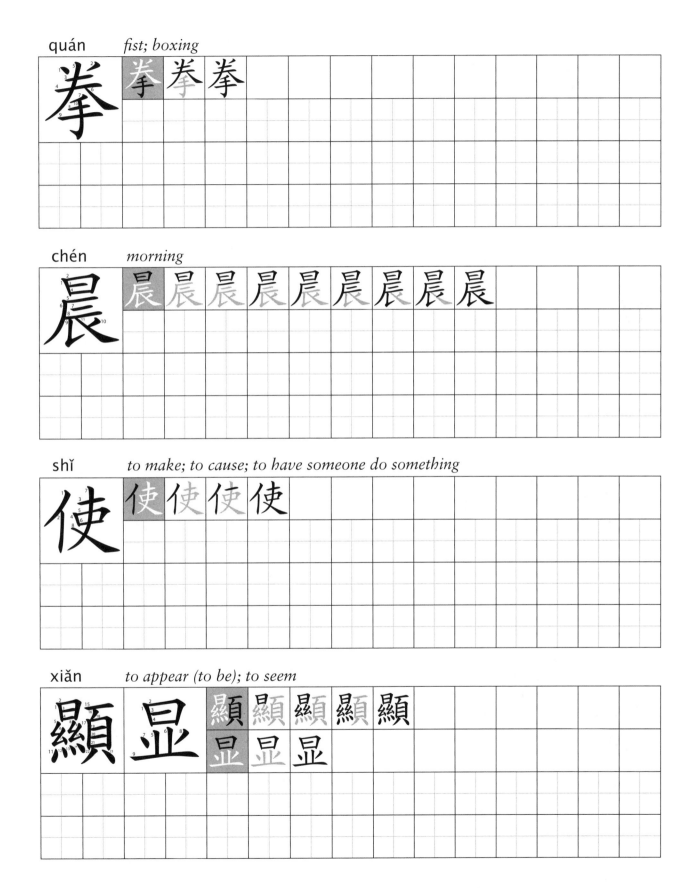

quán   *fist; boxing*

拳

chén   *morning*

晨

shǐ   *to make; to cause; to have someone do something*

使

xiǎn   *to appear (to be); to seem*

顯 显

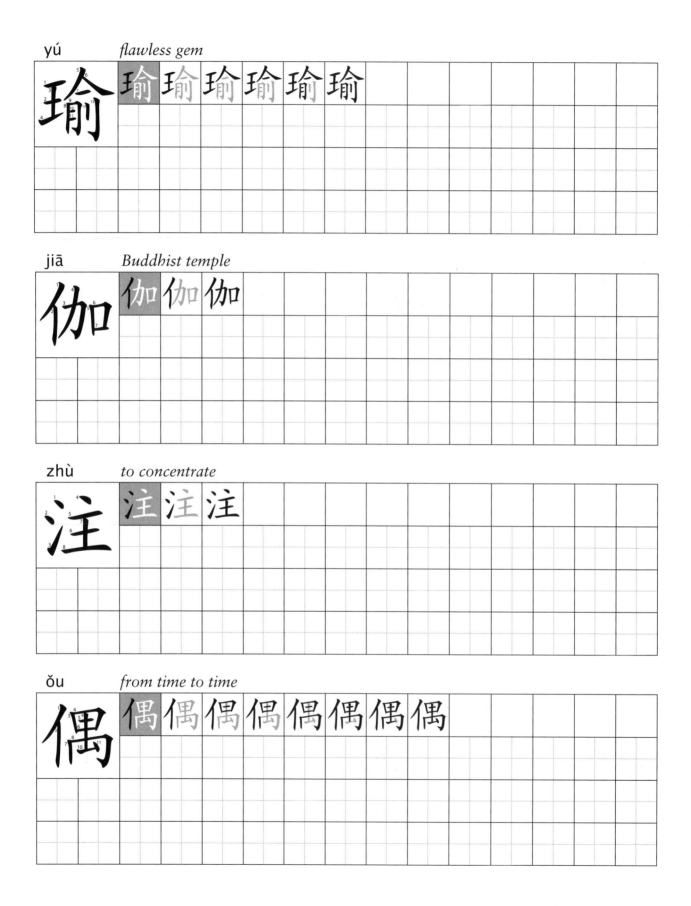

yú   *flawless gem*

瑜

jiā   *Buddhist temple*

伽

zhù   *to concentrate*

注

ǒu   *from time to time*

偶

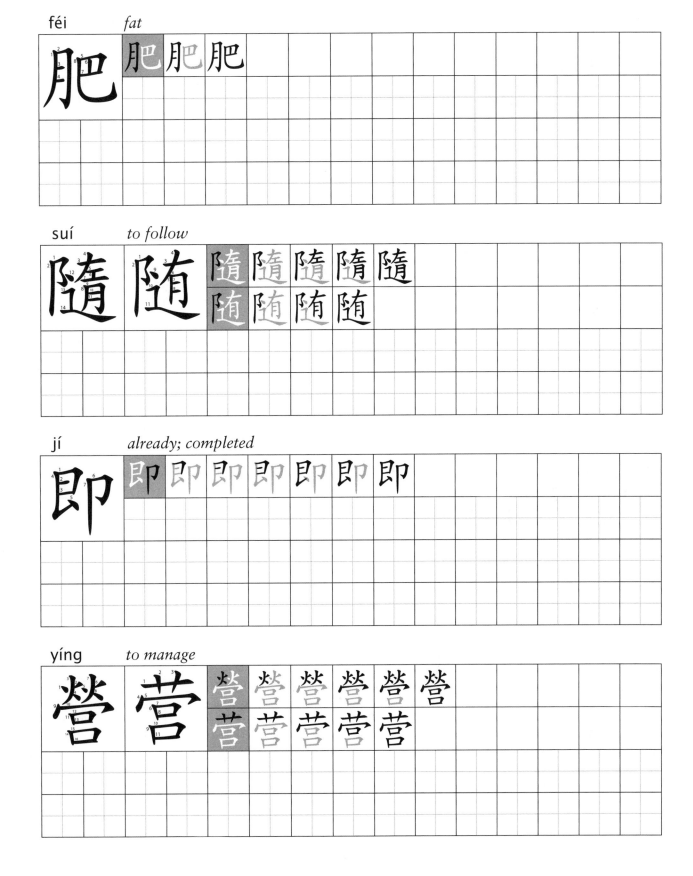

féi   *fat*

肥

suí   *to follow*

隨

jí   *already; completed*

即

yíng   *to manage*

營

bǎo   *full; satiated (after a meal)*

飽 饱 饱 饱 饱
饱 饱 饱

xī   *to inhale*

吸 吸 吸 吸

yān   *smoke; cigarette*

煙 烟 煙 煙 煙 煙
烟 烟 烟

áo   *to boil; to stew; to endure*

熬 熬 熬 熬 熬 熬

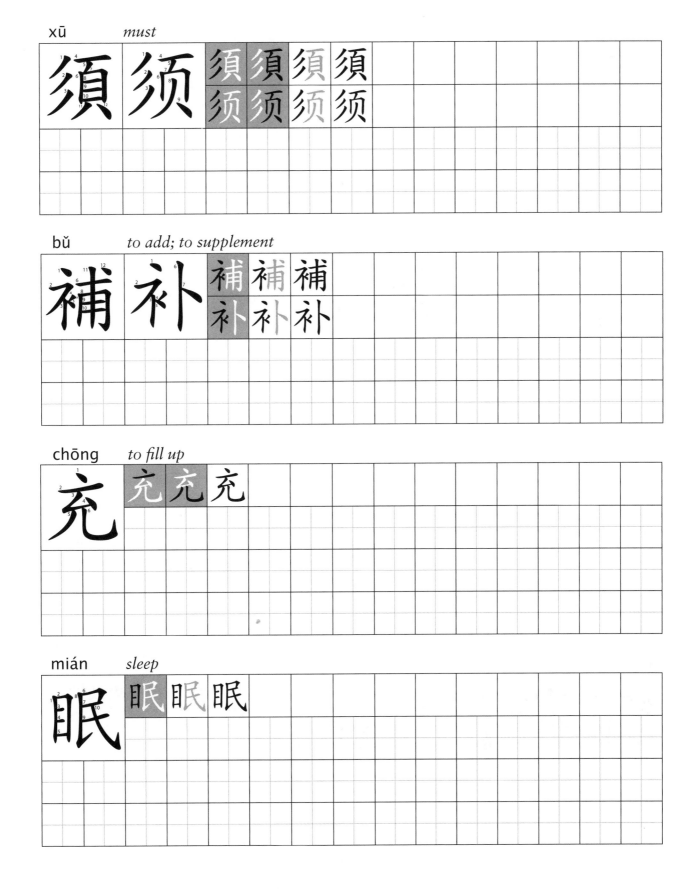

xū   *must*

須 须

bǔ   *to add; to supplement*

補 补

chōng   *to fill up*

充

mián   *sleep*

眠

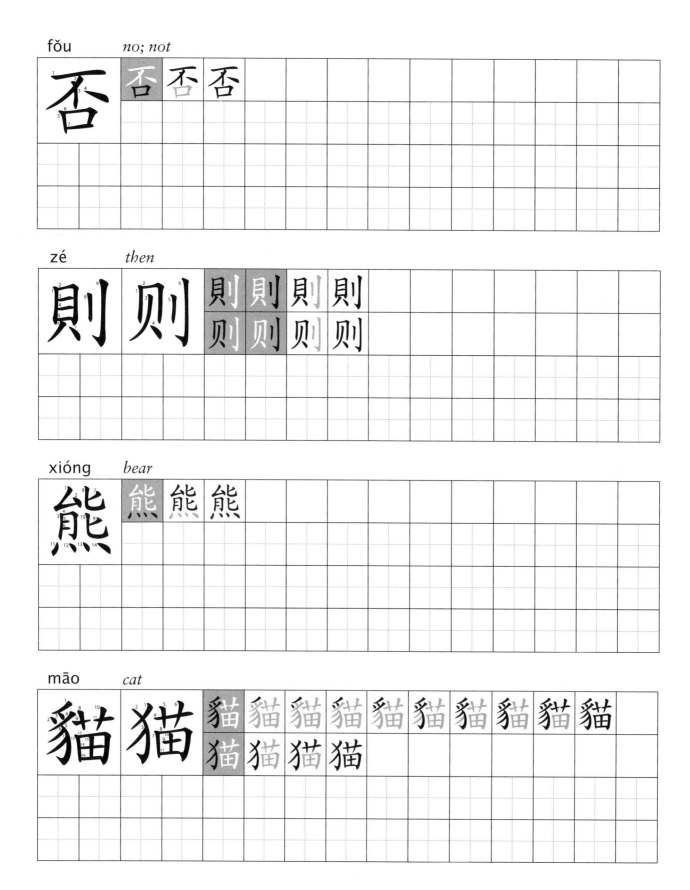

Chinese Character Crosswords

Fill out the puzzles based on the *pinyin* clues provided. The common character is positioned in the center of the cluster of rings. The arrows indicate which way you should read the words.

1.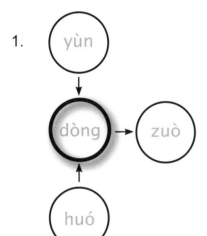

2.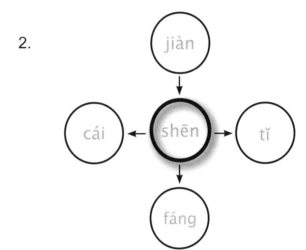

3.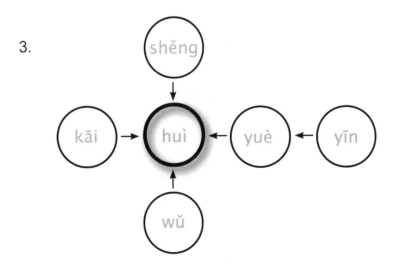

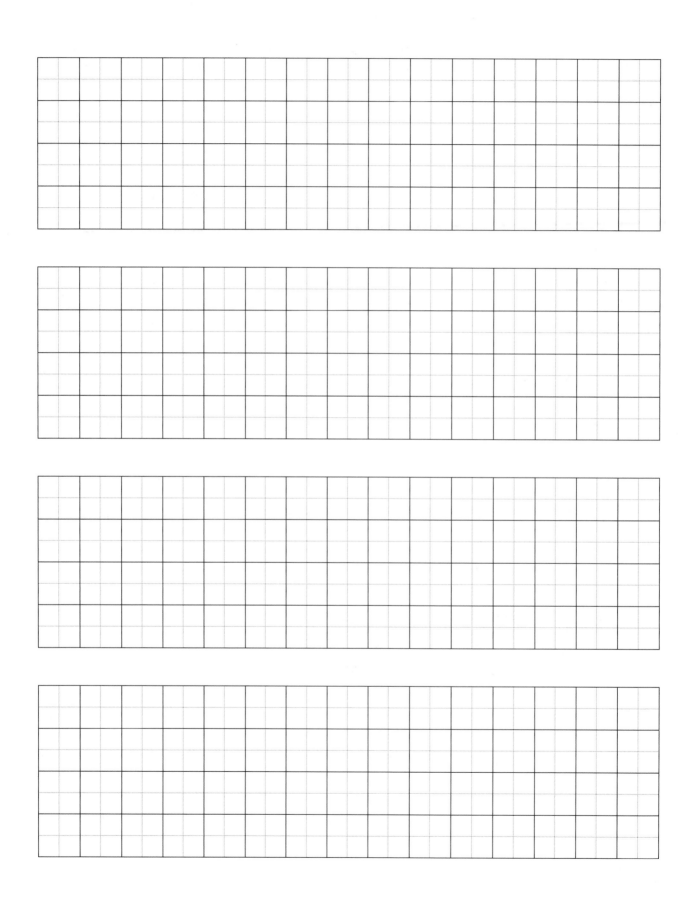

Lesson 15

fù   *woman*

婦 妇

kuàng   *circumstance; condition*

況 况

zhú   *one by one*

逐

jiàn   *gradually*

漸 渐

gǎi   *to change; to reform*

gé   *to transform*

mǒu   *certain; some; an indefinite person or thing*

qǐ   *to stand on tiptoe*

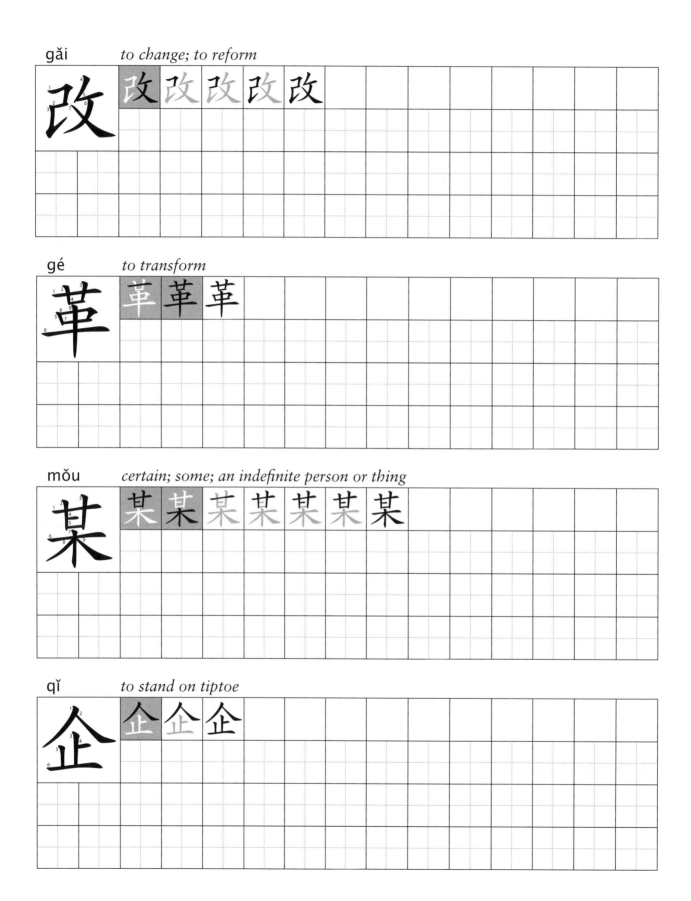

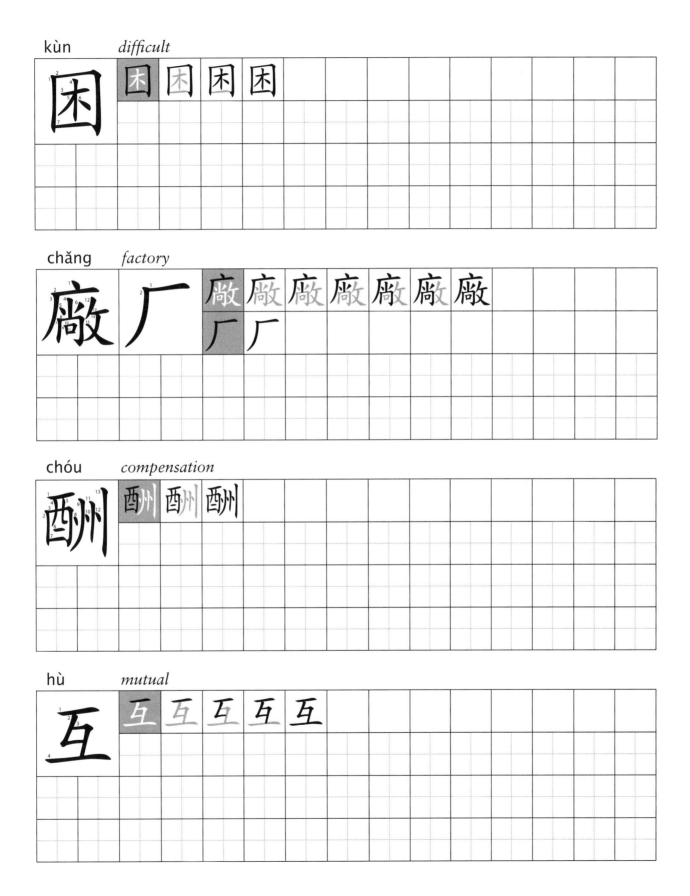

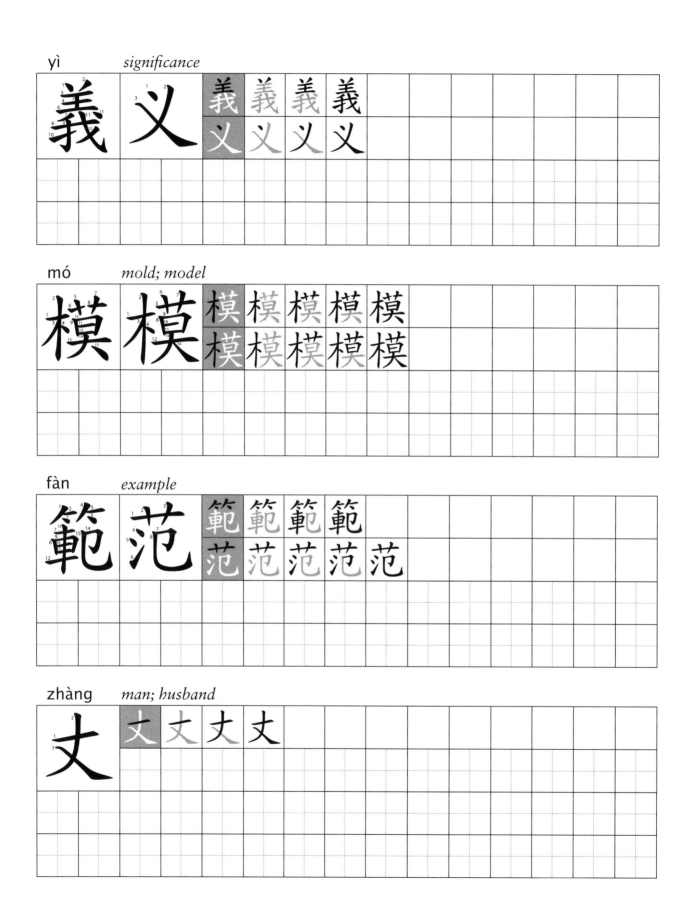

yì   *significance*

mó   *mold; model*

fàn   *example*

zhàng   *man; husband*

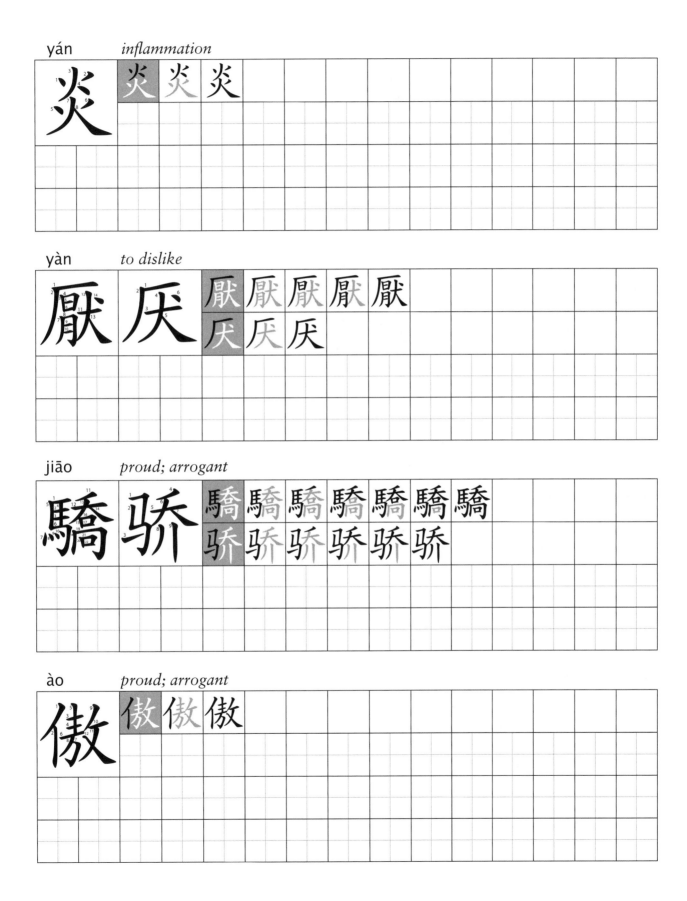

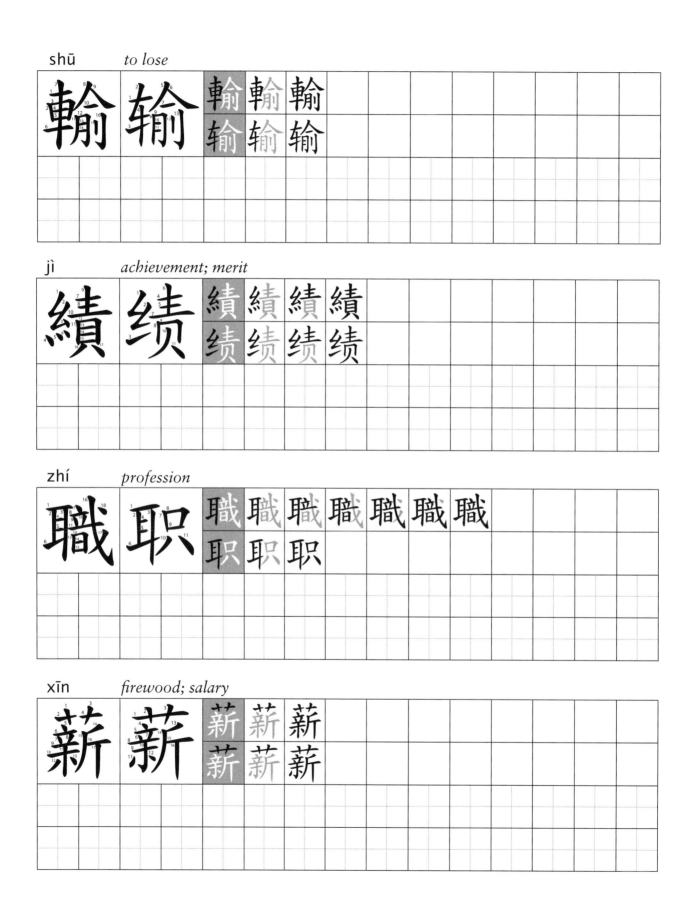

shū   *to lose*

jì   *achievement; merit*

zhí   *profession*

xīn   *firewood; salary*

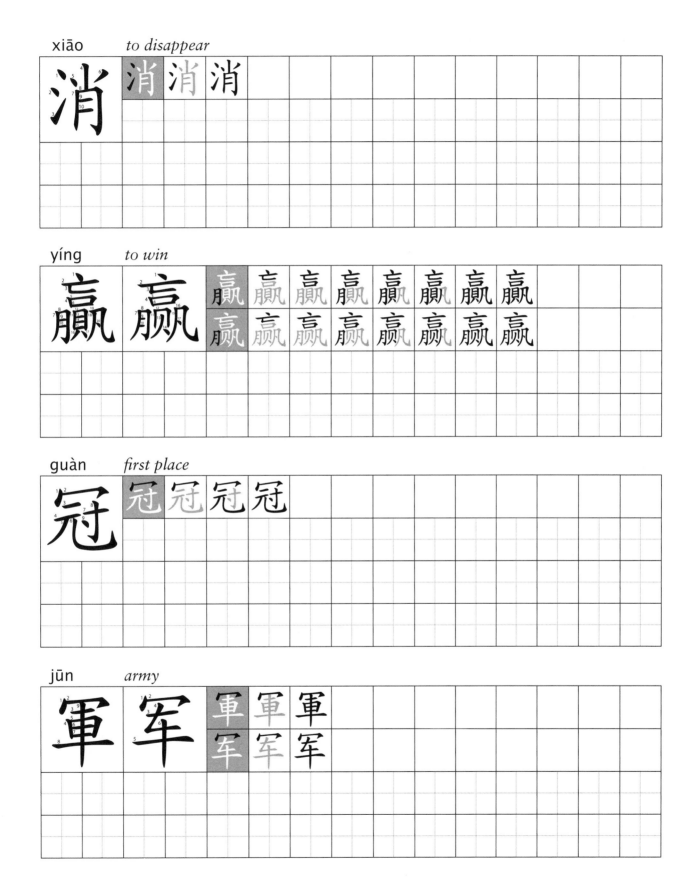

xiāo   *to disappear*

消

yíng   *to win*

赢

guàn   *first place*

冠

jūn   *army*

軍 军

pīng *sharp, high-pitched sound; ping*

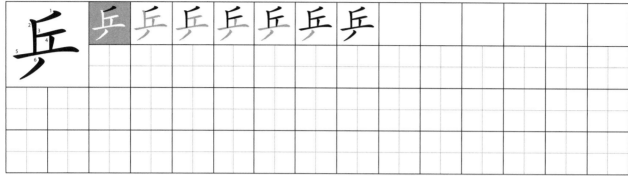

pāng *banging sound*

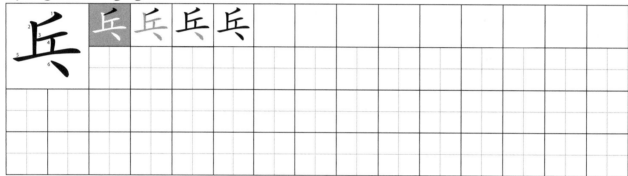

Character from Proper Nouns

bā *to hope anxiously*

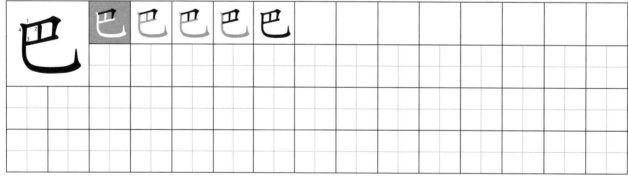

Chinese Character Crosswords

Fill out the puzzles based on the *pinyin* clues provided. The common character is positioned in the center of the cluster of rings. The arrows indicate which way you should read the words.

1.
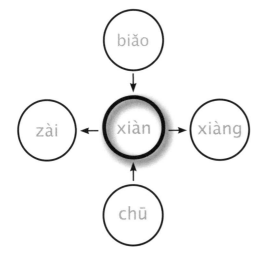

2.
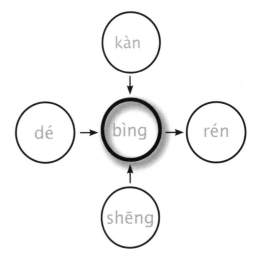

3.
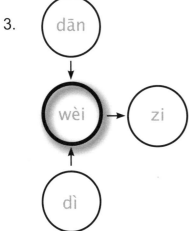

4.
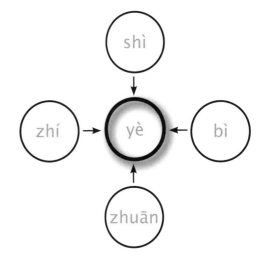

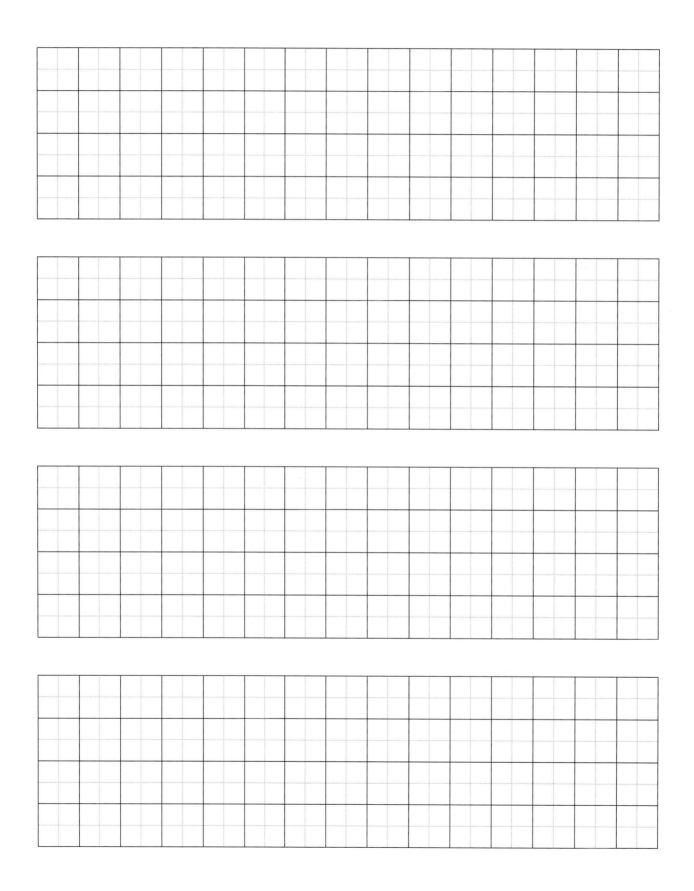

Lesson 16

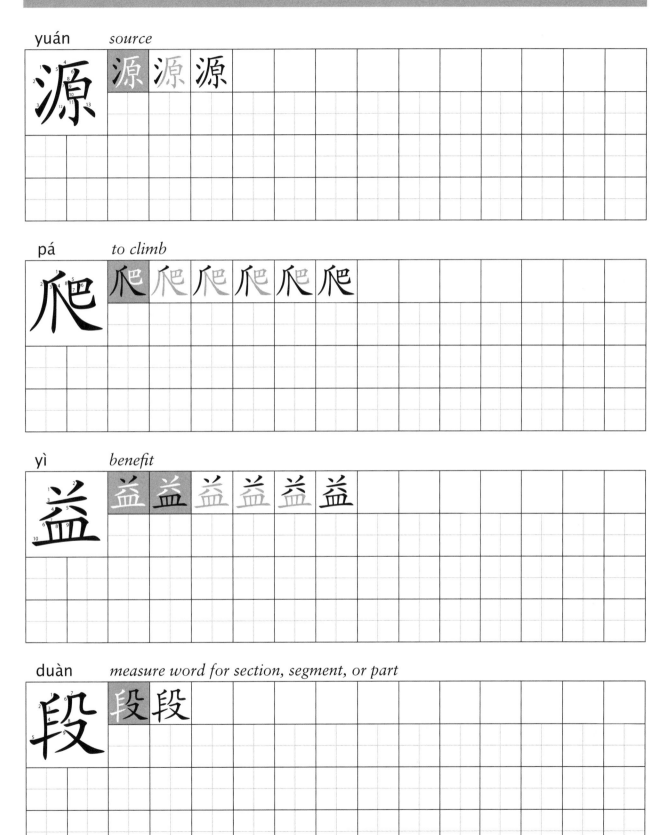

yuán   *source*

源

pá   *to climb*

爬

yì   *benefit*

益

duàn   *measure word for section, segment, or part*

段

tuī   *to push; to shove*

tǒng   *thick tube-shaped object*

rēng   *to throw; to toss; to throw away*

yáng   *sun*

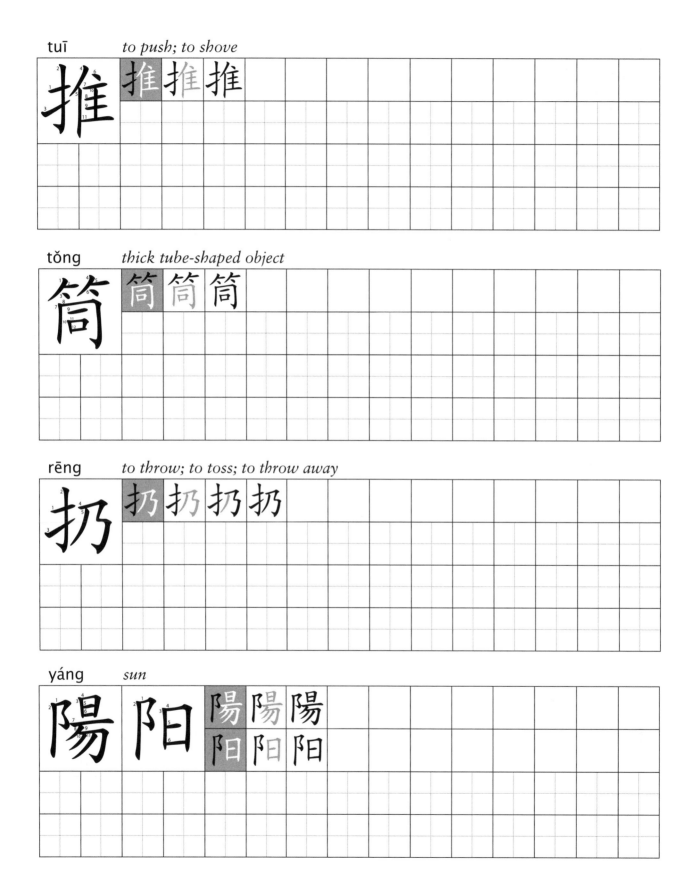

méi   *coal*

煤 煤 煤 煤

guī   *rule*

規 规 规 规 规 规 规 规 规 规

wēn   *warm*

温 温 温 温 温

shè   *to take in; to absorb*

攝 摄 摄 摄 摄 摄 摄 摄 摄 摄

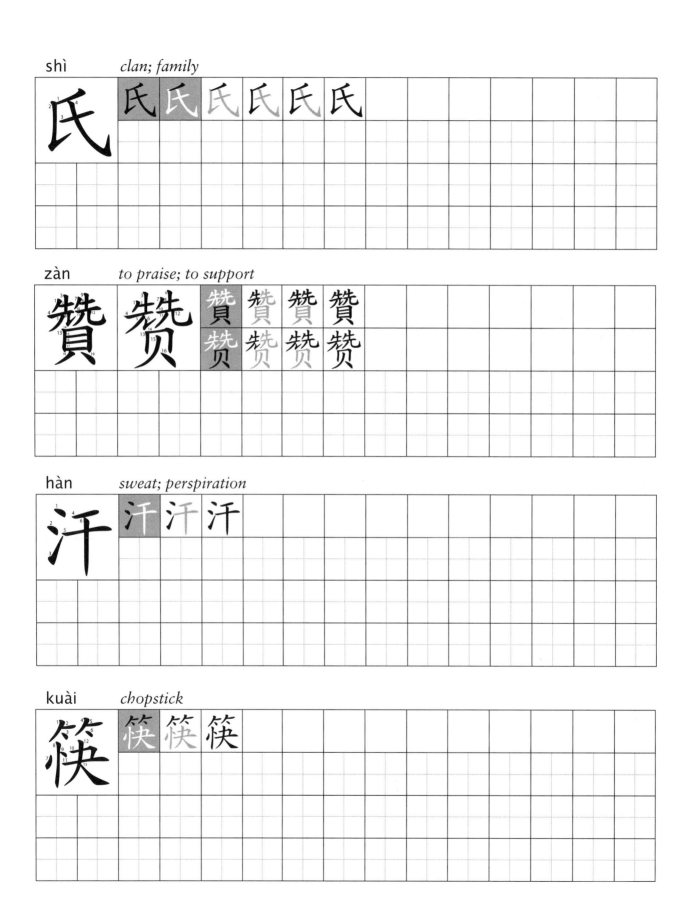

shì   *clan; family*

氏

zàn   *to praise; to support*

赞

hàn   *sweat; perspiration*

汗

kuài   *chopstick*

筷

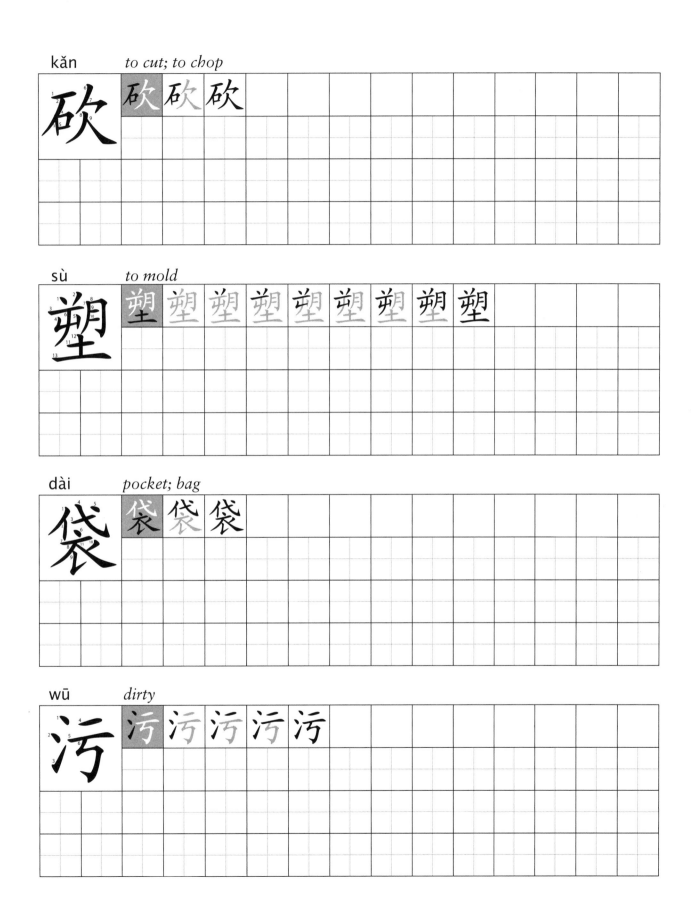

kǎn   *to cut; to chop*
砍 砍 砍 砍

sù   *to mold*
塑 塑 塑 塑 塑 塑 塑 塑 塑

dài   *pocket; bag*
袋 袋 袋 袋

wū   *dirty*
污 污 污 污 污

rǎn   *to dye*

zào   *to make; to cause*

kān   *to be capable of; to be worthy of*

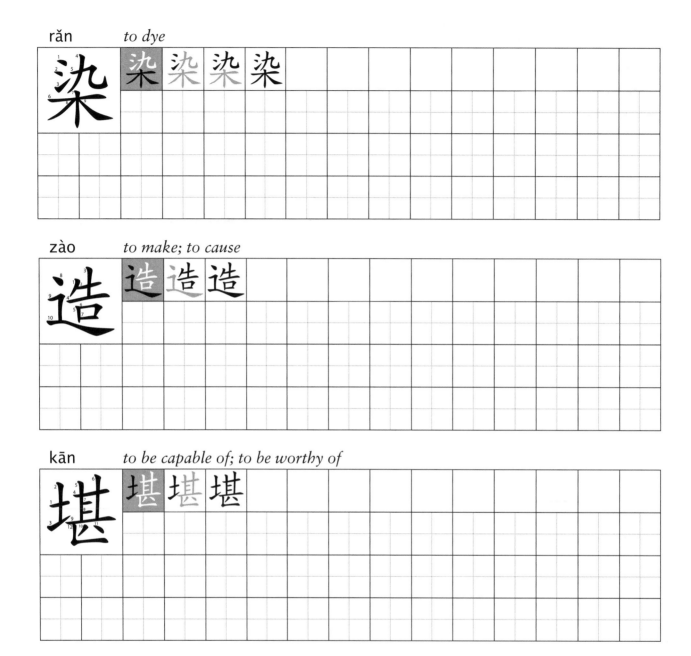

Character from Proper Nouns

kè   *to overcome*

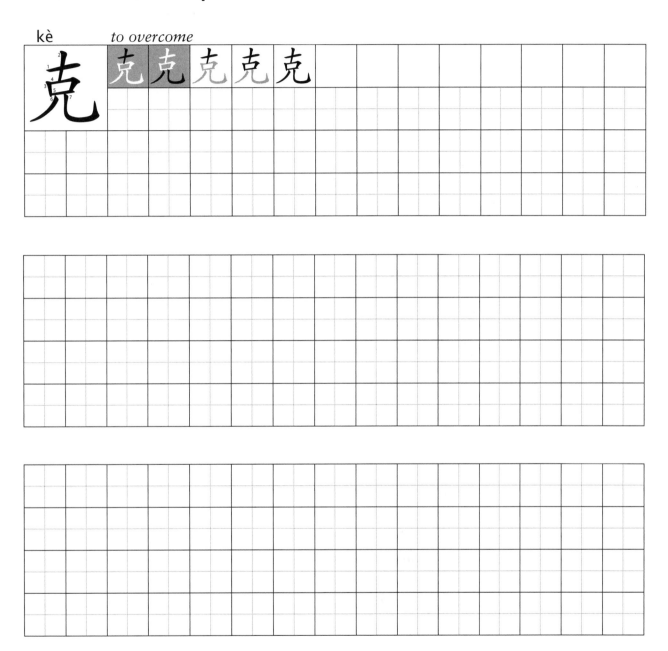

Chinese Character Crosswords

Fill out the puzzles based on the *pinyin* clues provided. The common character is positioned in the center of the cluster of rings. The arrows indicate which way you should read the words.

1.
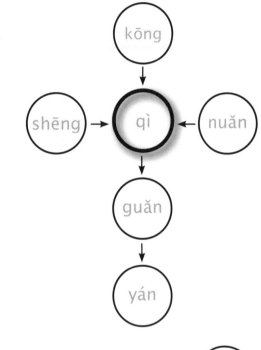

2.
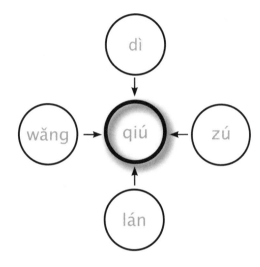

3.
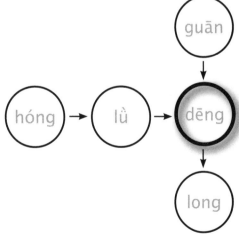

tóu   *to throw; to cast*

投 | 投 投 投

zēng   *to increase*

增 | 增 增 增 增 增 增 增 增

xiàng   *direction; toward*

向 | 向 向 向 向

jiǎn   *temperate; frugal*

儉 儉 | 儉 儉 儉 / 儉 儉 儉

zhǎng   *(of water, prices, etc.) to rise; to surge; to go up*

漲　漲　漲　漲　漲
　　　　　漲　漲　漲

chǎo   *to saute; to stir-fry; to speculate (for profit)*

炒　炒　炒　炒

gǔ   *thigh; share (of stock)*

股　股　股　股

yǐn   *to draw out; to attract*

引　引　引　引

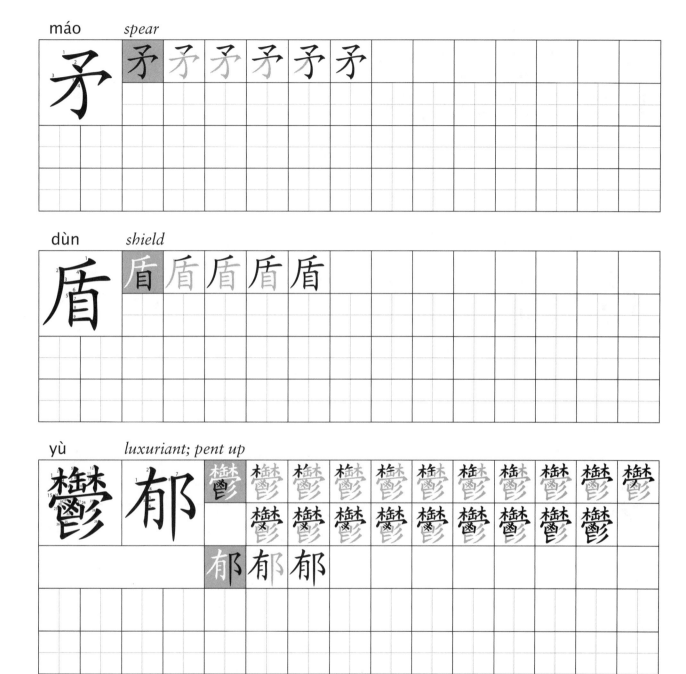

máo   *spear*

矛

dùn   *shield*

盾

yù   *luxuriant; pent up*

鬱 郁

mèn   *depressed*

sūn   *grandchild*

wèi   *not yet*

quàn   *to persuade; to advise; to urge*

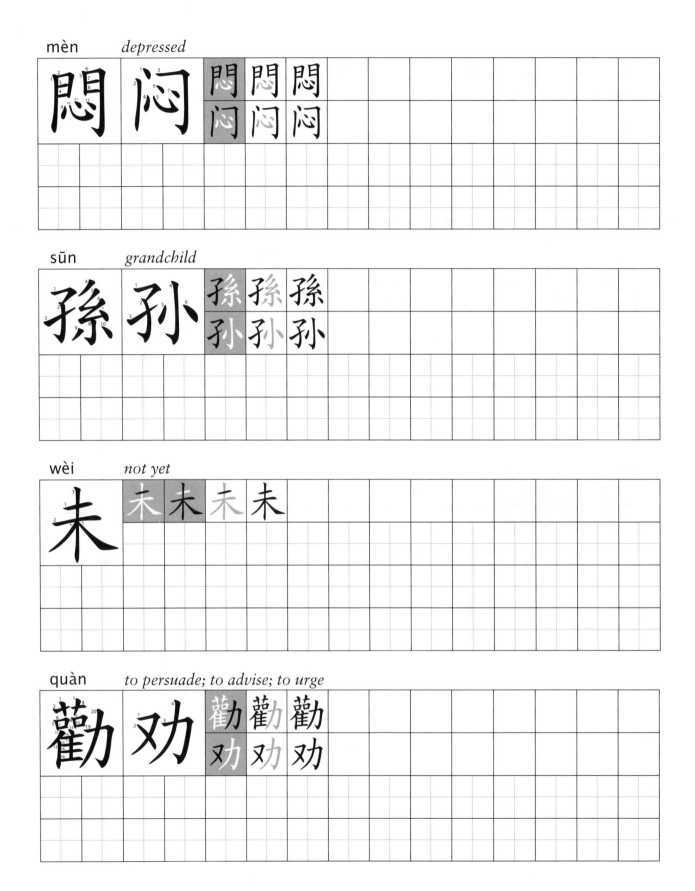

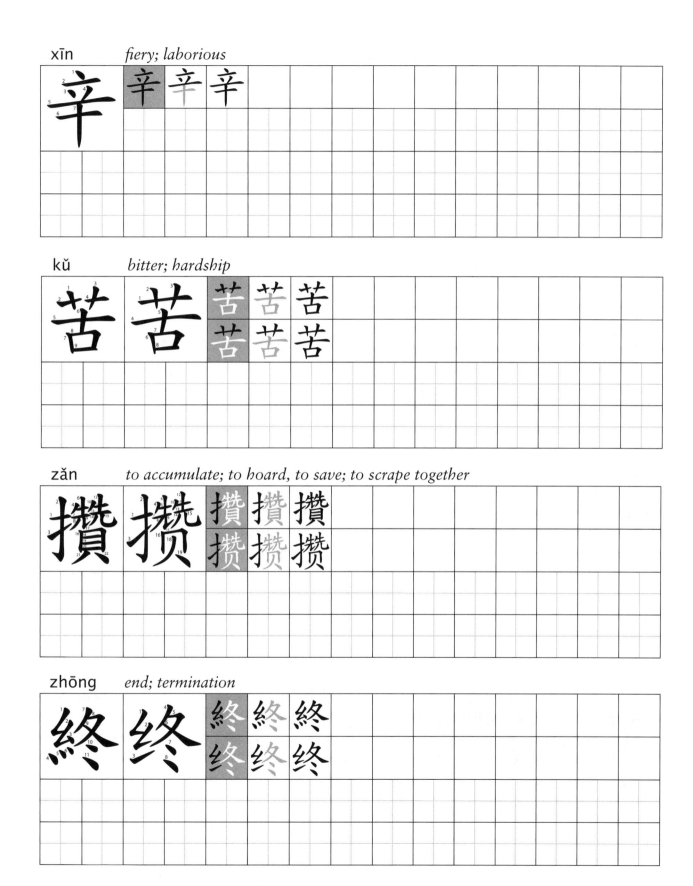

xīn   *fiery; laborious*

kǔ   *bitter; hardship*

zǎn   *to accumulate; to hoard, to save; to scrape together*

zhōng   *end; termination*

tū   *to break through; to protrude; sudden*

突   突 突 突

dǐ   *to resist; to offset*

抵   抵 抵 抵

diē   *to fall*

跌   跌 跌 跌 跌 跌 跌

péi   *to lose (money, etc.); to suffer a loss in a deal*

赔 赔   赔 赔 赔 赔   赔 赔 赔 赔

Chinese Character Crosswords

Fill out the puzzles based on the *pinyin* clues provided. The common character is positioned in the center of the cluster of rings. The arrows indicate which way you should read the words.

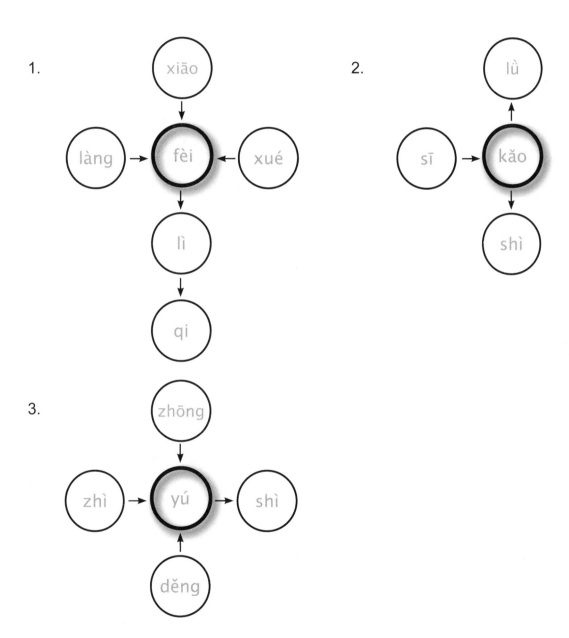

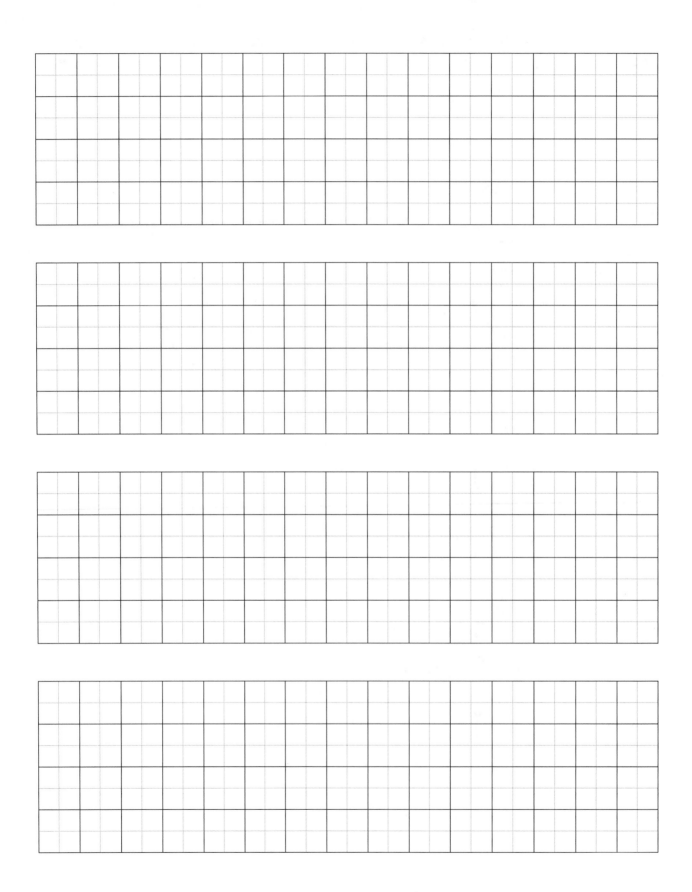

Lesson 18

guān   *to view*

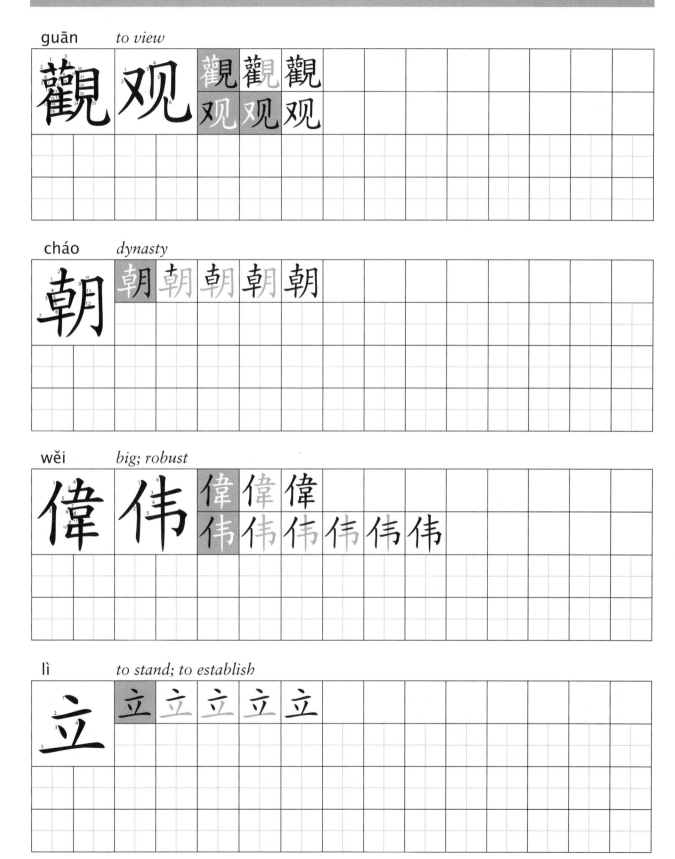

cháo   *dynasty*

wěi   *big; robust*

lì   *to stand; to establish*

zhǎn   *to unfold*

展   展 展 展 展 展 展 展

huáng   *emperor; imperial*

皇   皇 皇 皇

dì   *emperor*

帝   帝 帝 帝 帝 帝 帝 帝

gòng   *to offer tribute*

貢 贡   貢 貢 貢 貢 / 贡 贡 贡 贡

xiàn *to offer; to present*

獻 献 獻獻獻獻獻獻獻獻獻獻
献献献

xiū *to build; to repair; to mend; to fix*

修 修修修修修

shā *to kill*

殺 杀 殺殺殺殺殺
杀杀杀

gōng *palace*

宫 宫 宫宫宫宫
宫宫宫宫

diàn   *hall; palace*

殿　殿 殿 殿 殿

fén   *tomb; mound*

墳 坟　墳 墳 墳 墳 墳
　　　坟 坟 坟

mù   *grave*

墓 墓　墓 墓 墓 墓 墓 墓
　　　墓 墓 墓 墓 墓 墓

bīng   *soldier*

兵　兵 兵 兵 兵

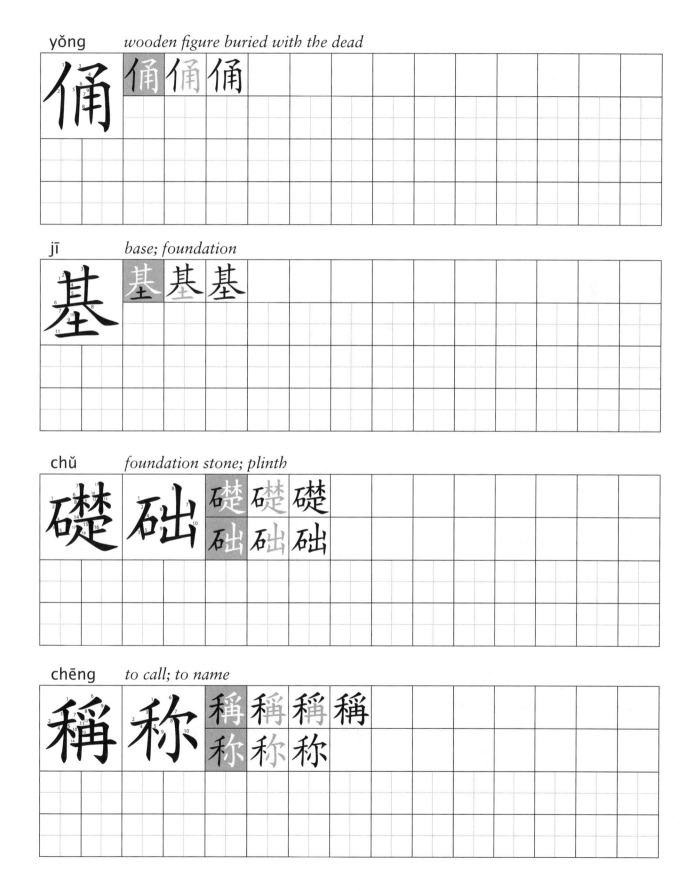

yǒng — *wooden figure buried with the dead*

jī — *base; foundation*

chǔ — *foundation stone; plinth*

chēng — *to call; to name*

sī   *silk*

chóu   *silk cloth*

mào   *to trade; to barter*

shī   *poetry; poem*

Lesson 19

kuà   *to cross; to straddle*

跨

fēn   *numerous; in great profusion*

紛 纷

guī   *to return*

歸 归

cǐ   *this*

此

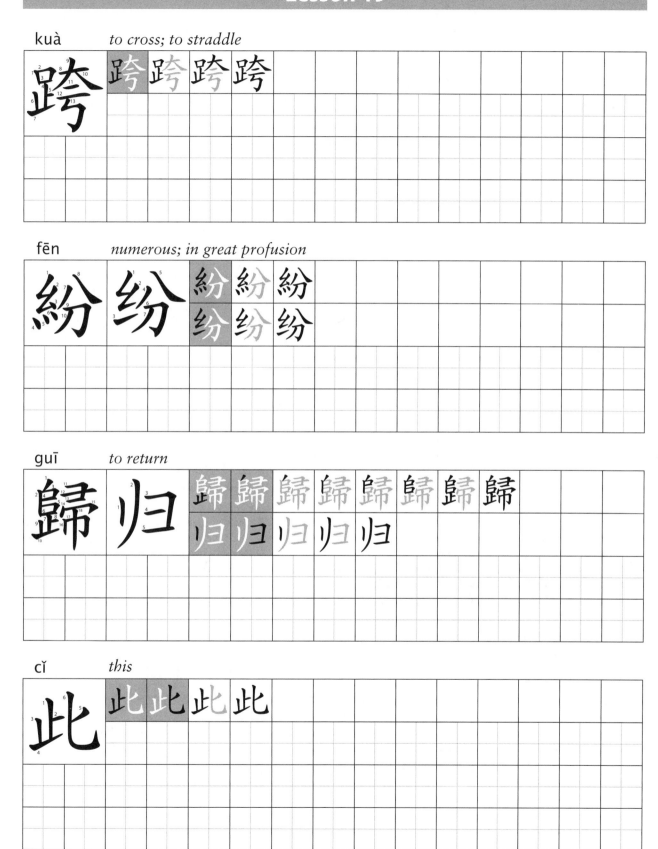

guī   *turtle; tortoise*

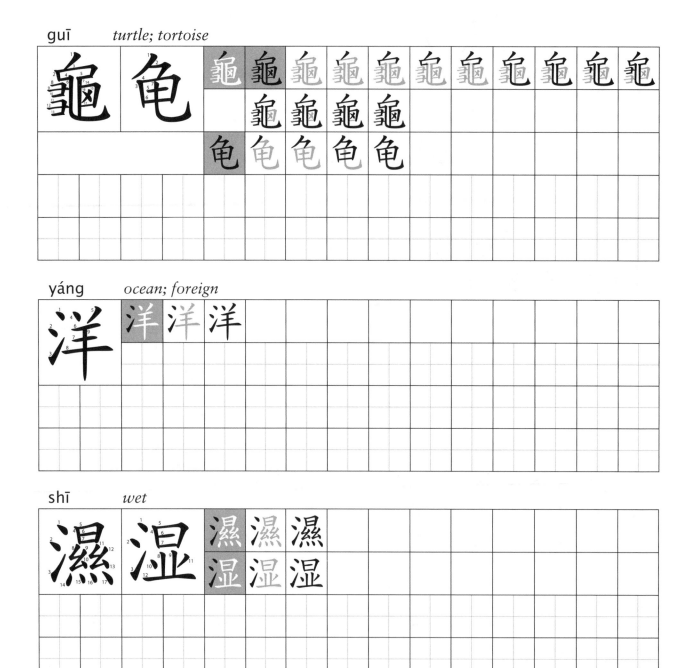

yáng   *ocean; foreign*

shī   *wet*

vessel; machine

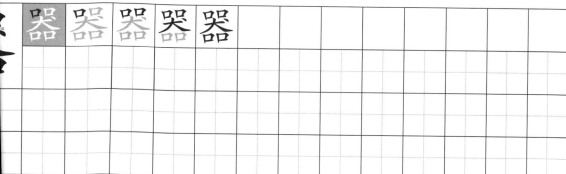

drama

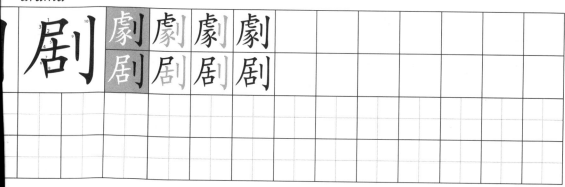

to do; to carry on; to be engaged in

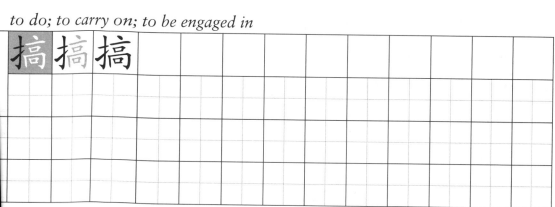

value; to be worthy

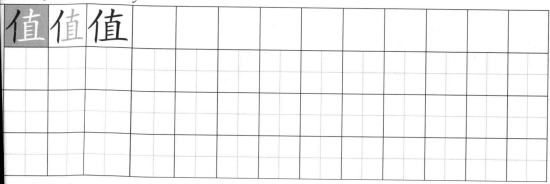

shàn   *good; kind*

wò   *to hold; to grasp*

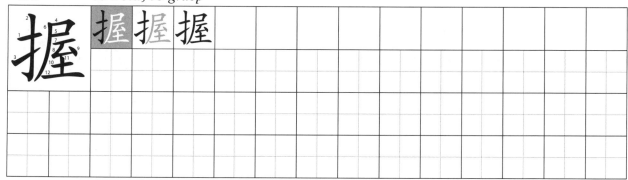

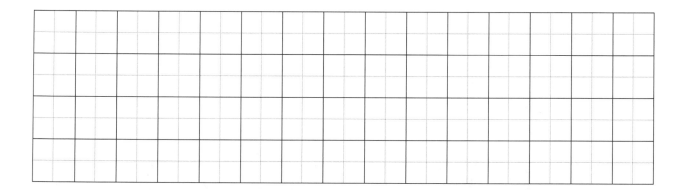

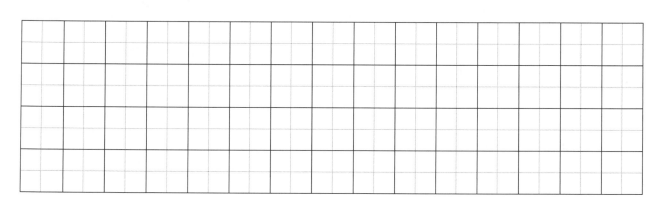

Chinese Character Crosswords

Fill out the puzzles based on the *pinyin* clues provided. The common character is positioned in the center of the cluster of rings. The arrows indicate which way you should read the words.

1.
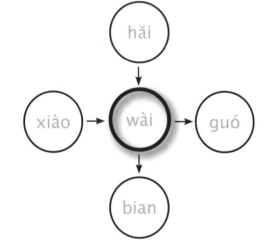

2.
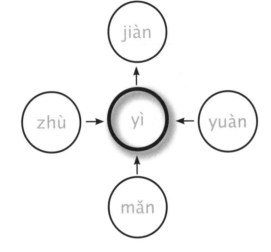

3.
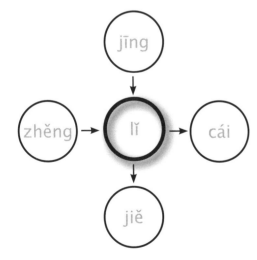

4.
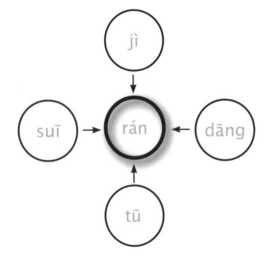

Integrated Chinese

Lesson 20

jù   *to gather together*

qìng   *to celebrate*

jiàn   *to give a farewell party; preserved food*

guō   *wok; pot*

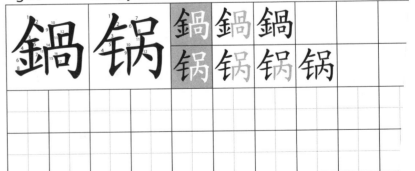

qì

jù

gǎo

zhí

wěn　*stable*

稳　稳　稳　稳　稳　稳　稳　稳
　　　　稳　稳　稳

jǐn　*only*

僅　仅　僅　僅　僅　僅　僅　僅
　　　仅　仅　仅

yǒng　*always; forever*

永　永　永　永　永　永　永

lián　*to link; to connect*

聯　联　聯　聯　聯
　　　联　联　联

yì   *friendship*

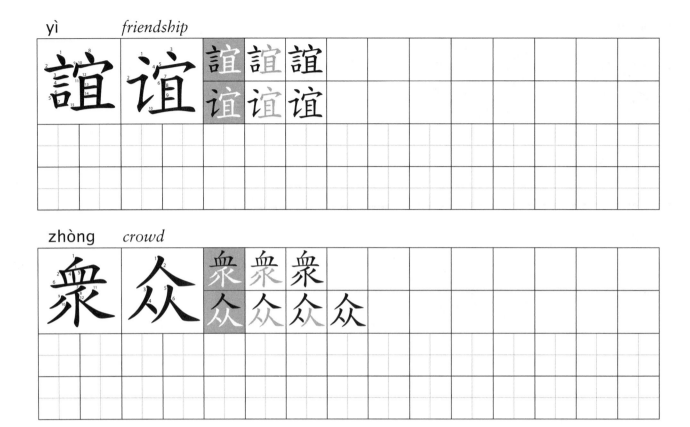

zhòng   *crowd*

Characters from Proper Nouns

Ōu   *a surname*

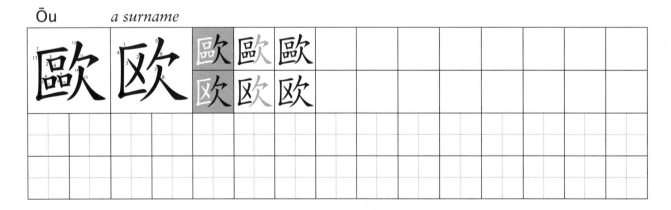

INDEX A
Characters by Pinyin

P = pinyin
T = traditional form
S = simplified form
L = lesson

gǎi	改		to change; to reform	15	42
gài	蓋	盖	to build; to construct	12	15
gǎo	搞		to do; to carry on; to be engaged in	20	86
gé	革		to transform	15	42
gōng	恭		respectful	11	8
gōng	宮	宫	palace	18	69
gòng	貢	贡	to offer tribute	18	68
gū	姑		father's sister	12	13
gū	咕		to mumble; to rumble	12	17
gǔ	股		thigh; share (of stock)	17	60
gù	故		ancient; former	13	26
guān	觀	观	to view	18	67
guàn	慣	惯	habit	13	25
guàn	冠		first place	15	47
guī	規	规	rule	16	53
guī	歸	归	to return	19	77
guī	龜	龟	turtle; tortoise	19	78
guō	鍋	锅	wok; pot	20	85
hàn	汗		sweat; perspiration	16	54
hé	盒		box	13	23
hū	呼	呼	to exhale	13	23
hù	互		mutual	15	43
huá	華	华	flowery; Chinese; China	18	75
huán	環	环	ring; to surround	11	2
huáng	皇		emperor; imperial	18	68
jī	基		base; foundation	18	71
jí	及		to reach; to come up to	12	13
jí	即		already; completed	14	35
jì	繼	继	to follow	11	1
jì	紀	纪	record; annal	13	27
jì	績	绩	achievement; merit	15	46
jì	技		skill	18	73
jì	寄		to mail	19	81
jì	既		already	19	81
jiā	伽		Buddhist temple	14	34
jiǎn	儉	俭	temperate; frugal	17	59
jiàn	漸	渐	gradually	15	41
jiàn	餞	饯	to give a farewell party; preserved food	20	85
jiǎng	講	讲	to speak; to tell	13	26
jiāo	驕	骄	proud; arrogant	15	45
jiē	街		street	12	14
jǐn	儘	尽	to exhaust	12	16
jǐn	僅	仅	only	20	87
jìng	境		territory	11	2
jìng	竟		unexpectedly; contrary to one's expectation	12	13
jiǔ	酒		alcohol; liquor	11	4
jiù	舅		mother's brother; maternal uncle	11	1
jǔ	舉	举	to lift; to raise	11	5
jù	聚		to gather together	20	85
jù	劇	剧	drama	20	86
jūn	軍	军	army	15	47
kān	堪		to be capable of; to be worthy of	16	56
kǎn	砍		to cut; to chop	16	55
kè	克		to overcome	16	57
kǒng	孔		opening; hole; a surname	18	74
kǔ	苦	苦	bitter; hardship	17	63
kuà	跨		to cross; to straddle	19	77
kuài	筷		chopstick	16	54
kuàng	況	况	circumstance; condition	15	41
kūn	昆		elder brother; descendant	13	28
kùn	困		difficult	15	43

shēng	聲	声	sound	12	17
shú	熟		cooked; familiar	12	14
xī	悉		to know	12	14
zhù	築	筑	to construct	12	16
zhuāng	裝	装	clothing	12	16
zuò	座		(measure word for buildings and mountains)	12	17
cān	參	参	to participate	13	21
dòu	逗		to tease; to play with; amusing	13	24
dùn	頓	顿	measure word for meals	13	23
gù	故		ancient; former	13	26
guàn	慣	惯	habit	13	25
hé	盒		box	13	23
hū	呼		to exhale	13	23
jì	紀	纪	record; annal	13	27
jiǎng	講	讲	to speak; to tell	13	26
kūn	昆		elder brother; descendant	13	28
kuò	括		to include	13	21
lǎn	覽	览	to view	13	25
lóng	籠	笼	cage	13	27
mò	默		silent	13	24
pù	鋪	铺	bunk	13	22
qīn	親	亲	relatives; self	13	24
shí	石		stone	13	25
shù	樹	树	tree	13	26
sú	俗		custom	13	25
tǎ	塔	塔	tower; pagoda-shaped structure	13	26
tōng	通		to pass through	13	21
wàn	萬	万	ten thousand	13	27
xiāng	廂	厢	side room; compartment	13	22
xiǎng	享		to enjoy	13	21
yìng	硬		hard	13	22
yōng	擁	拥	to embrace	13	23
yōu	幽		dark; secluded	13	24
zhěn	枕		pillow	13	22
áo	熬		to boil; to stew; to endure	14	36
bǎo	飽	饱	full; satiated (after a meal)	14	36
bǔ	補	补	to add; to supplement	14	37
chén	晨		morning	14	33
chōng	充		to fill up	14	37
duàn	鍛	锻	to forge; to temper	14	32
duì	隊	队	a row or line of people; column; (measure word for teams and lines)	14	32
féi	肥		fat	14	35
fǒu	否		no; not	14	38
jí	即		already; completed	14	35
jiā	伽		Buddhist temple	14	34
liàn	煉	炼	to smelt; to refine	14	32
māo	貓	猫	cat	14	38
mián	眠		sleep	14	37
ǒu	偶		from time to time	14	34
qī	妻		wife	14	31
quān	圈		circle; to encircle; to mark with a circle	14	32
quán	拳		fist; boxing	14	33
sàn	散		to scatter	14	31
shǐ	使		to make; to cause; to have someone do something	14	33
suí	隨	随	to follow	14	35
tuì	退		to retreat	14	31
xī	吸		to inhale	14	36
xiǎn	顯	显	to appear (to be); to seem	14	33
xióng	熊		bear	14	38
xū	須	须	must	14	37
yān	煙	烟	smoke; cigarette	14	36
yíng	營	营	to manage	14	35
yú	瑜		flawless gem	14	34

Pinyin	Traditional	Simplified	Definition		
yǔ	與	与	and; with	14	31
zé	則	则	then	14	38
zhù	注		to concentrate	14	34
ào	傲		proud; arrogant	15	45
bā	巴		to hope anxiously	15	48
chǎng	廠	厂	factory	15	43
chóu	酬		compensation	15	43
fàn	範	范	example	15	44
fù	婦	妇	woman	15	41
gǎi	改		to change; to reform	15	42
gé	革		to transform	15	42
guàn	冠		first place	15	47
hù	互		mutual	15	43
jì	績	绩	achievement; merit	15	46
jiàn	漸	渐	gradually	15	41
jiāo	驕	骄	proud; arrogant	15	45
jūn	軍	军	army	15	47
kuàng	況	况	circumstance; condition	15	41
kùn	困		difficult	15	43
mó	模	模	mold; model	15	44
mǒu	某		certain; some; an indefinite person or thing	15	42
pāng	乓		banging sound	15	48
pīng	乒		sharp, high-pitched sound; ping	15	48
qǐ	企		to stand on tiptoe	15	42
shū	輸	输	to lose	15	46
xiāo	消		to disappear	15	47
xīn	薪	薪	firewood; salary	15	46
yán	炎		inflammation	15	45
yàn	厭	厌	to dislike	15	45
yì	義	义	significance	15	44
yíng	贏	赢	to win	15	47
zhàng	丈		man; husband	15	44
zhí	職	职	profession	15	46
zhú	逐		one by one	15	41
dài	袋		pocket; bag	16	55
duàn	段		measure word for section, segment, or part	16	51
guī	規	规	rule	16	53
hàn	汗		sweat; perspiration	16	54
kān	堪		to be capable of; to be worthy of	16	56
kǎn	砍		to cut; to chop	16	55
kè	克		to overcome	16	57
kuài	筷		chopstick	16	54
méi	煤		coal	16	53
pá	爬		to climb	16	51
rǎn	染		to dye	16	56
rēng	扔		to throw; to toss; to throw away	16	52
shè	攝	摄	to take in; to absorb	16	53
shì	氏		clan; family	16	54
sù	塑		to mold	16	55
tǒng	筒		thick tube-shaped object	16	52
tuī	推		to push; to shove	16	52
wēn	溫		warm	16	53
wū	污		dirty	16	55
yáng	陽	阳	sun	16	52
yì	益		benefit	16	51
yuán	源		source	16	51
zàn	贊	赞	to praise; to support	16	54
zào	造		to make; to cause	16	56
chǎo	炒		to saute; to stir-fry; to speculate (for profit)	17	60
dǐ	抵		to resist; to offset	17	64
diē	跌		to fall	17	64
dùn	盾		shield	17	61
gǔ	股		thigh; share (of stock)	17	60
jiǎn	儉	俭	temperate; frugal	17	59